Waterside Walks in West London

PETER & CAROLYN STOTT

SPURBOOKS

Published by:
SPURBOOKS
(a division of Holmes McDougall Ltd.)
Allander House
Leith Walk
Edinburgh

© Peter & Carolyn Stott 1981

At the time of publication all the walks in this book were along paths designated as towpaths or official footpaths, but it should be borne in mind that diversion orders may be made from time to time, and neither the authors nor the publisher can accept responsibility for those who stray from the Rights of Way.

ISBN 0 7157 2096 1

All Rights Reserved: No part of this publication may be reproduced, stored in a retrieval system, or transmitted in any form or by any means, electronic, photocopying, recording or otherwise, without the prior permission of the publisher.

Printed and bound in Scotland
by McQueen, Galashiels
and Holmes McDougall Ltd., Edinburgh

CONTENTS

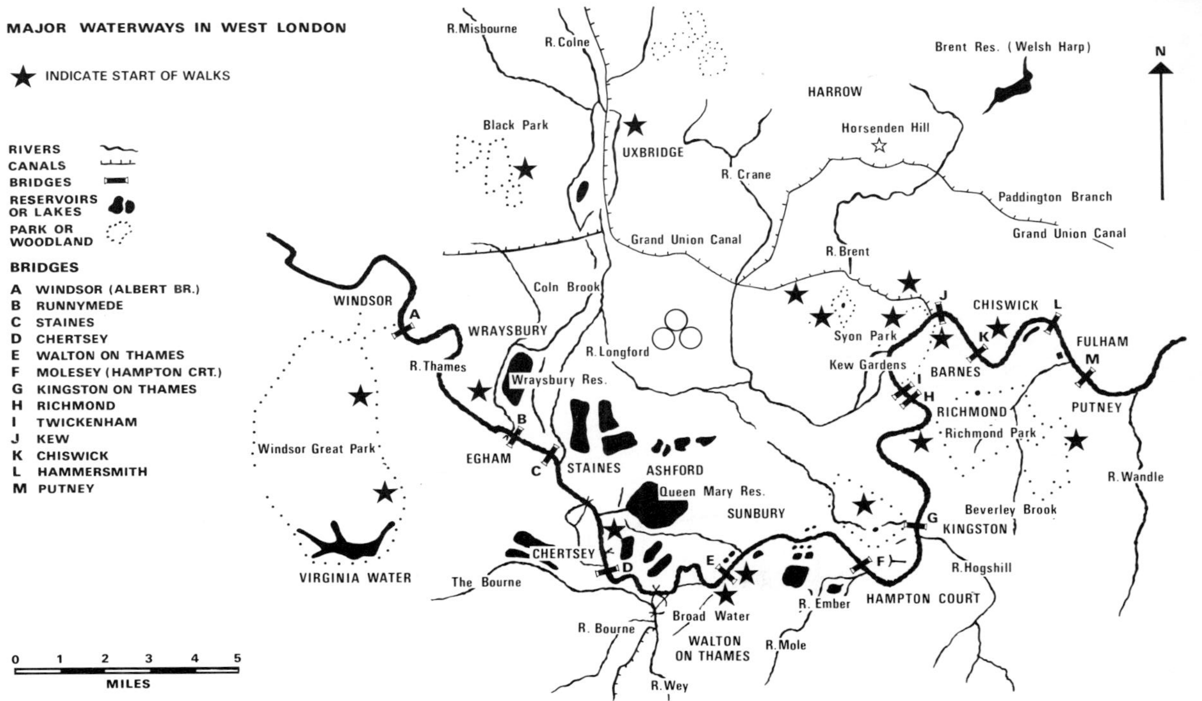

MAJOR WATERWAYS IN WEST LONDON
INDICATE START OF WALKS
RIVERS
CANALS
BRIDGES
RESERVOIRS OR LAKES
PARK OR WOODLAND
BRIDGES
A WINDSOR (ALBERT BR.)
B RUNNYMEDE
C STAINES
D CHERTSEY
E WALTON ON THAMES
F MOLESEY (HAMPTON CRT.)
G KINGSTON ON THAMES
H RICHMOND
I TWICKENHAM
J KEW
K CHISWICK
L HAMMERSMITH
M PUTNEY
0 1 2 3 4 5
MILES
N
R.Misbourne
R.Colne
Brent Res. (Welsh Harp)
HARROW
Black Park
Horsenden Hill
UXBRIDGE
R.Crane
Paddington Branch
Grand Union Canal
R.Brent
Grand Union Canal
Coln Brook
WINDSOR
WRAYSBURY
R.Longford
Syon Park
CHISWICK
Kew Gardens
BARNES
FULHAM
R.Thames
Wraysbury Res.
RICHMOND
PUTNEY
EGHAM
STAINES
ASHFORD
Richmond Park
R.Wandle
Windsor Great Park
Queen Mary Res.
SUNBURY
Beverley Brook
KINGSTON
VIRGINIA WATER
CHERTSEY
The Bourne
Broad Water
R.Ember
R.Hogshill
HAMPTON COURT
R.Bourne
WALTON ON THAMES
R.Mole
R.Wey

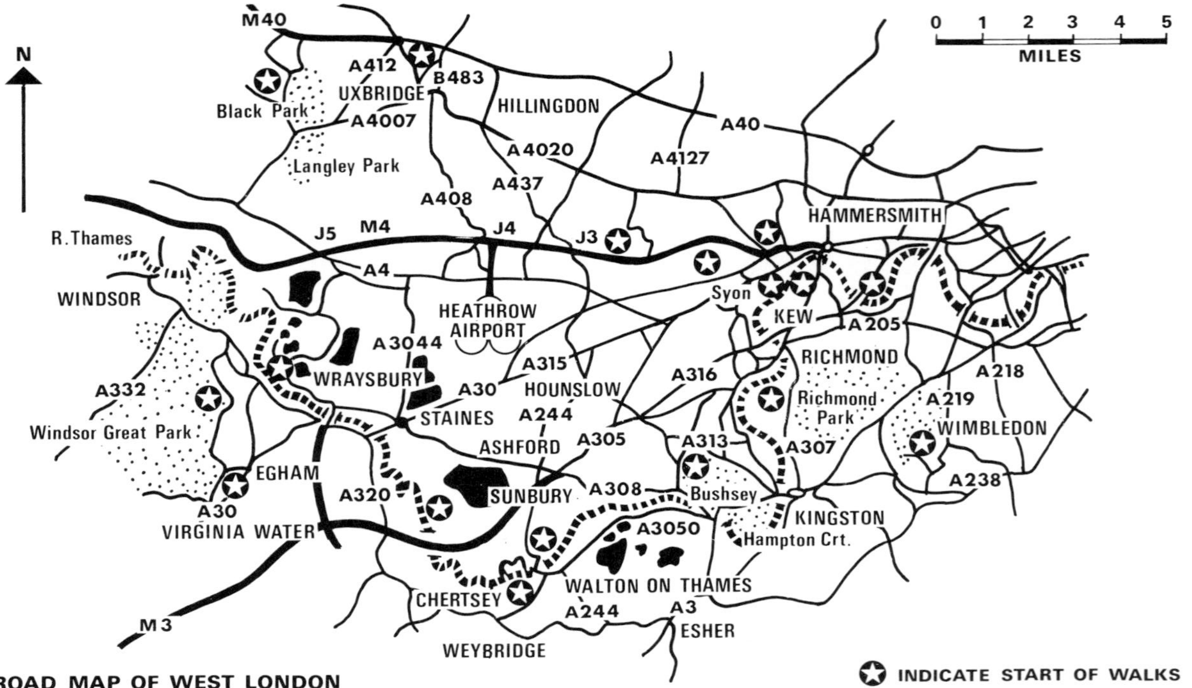

ROAD MAP OF WEST LONDON

6

INTRODUCTION

The western approaches to London are dominated by water and all the walks in this book are in some way associated with it. Over half are based upon the Thames and the remainder on either the Grand Union/Junction Canal or on one of the smaller rivers. The degree to which the development of this area has been influenced by its waterways will become obvious as you follow the walks.

The River Thames
The Thames was once known as 'The King's River'. In Tudor times it was the main highway, and boats were owned by all classes of people. The Thames Watermen and Lightermen, who piloted the small boats and who plied for hire, were a much respected body of men. However, during the eighteenth and early nineteenth centuries, Thames travel declined. With the explosion in London's population at this time, the river took on more and more of the character of an open sewer. It was not until 1856, when the stench reached Parliament's nostrils at Westminster, that proper sewerage was initiated in London. In the present century, conservation of the environment has become important, and more and more strict regulations have been imposed so that the river has once more become a source of pleasure. Since the mid-1960s, pollution and effluent control have been used so effectively that many fish, which were previously unable to survive in the water, are now returning to the Thames.

Above London, between 925 million and 1300 million gallons of water a day are abstracted from the Thames for household and industrial purposes. In the west of London the Metropolitan Water Authority has built many reservoirs, and in some of them experimental trout farms are in operation. Examples of these may be seen at Datchet and Barn Elms.

The Tideway, that part of the river which flows back and forth with the tides, stretches from the mouth up to Teddington Weir; the weir maintains a constant level of water above that point.

The Canals
In 1790, the Oxford Canal was opened. This ran northwards from the Thames at Oxford, linking London with the Midlands. However, there were no locks on the Thames below Staines until 1811, when Teddington Lock was built, and parts of the river were very hazardous. As a consequence this route to London was rather unpredictable. By 1800, the Grand Junction Canal (later to be known as the Grand Union Canal) was in operation. From London barges would use the Thames as far as Brentford and then join the canal itself. The steep sides of the Thames basin were traversed by means of the Hanwell lock series and then the canal followed the valley of the river Colne out towards the Midlands, in all a total length of 93 miles. A branch line from Southall to Paddington, connecting there with the Regent's Canal, was opened soon after and for some time was used to supply water to households in the Chelsea and Paddington areas.

In 1838, the railway era arrived. The London-to-Midlands route followed that of the canal very closely and took away much of its trade, thereby hastening its demise.

Among these rivers, canals, lakes and reservoirs, various people have built their homes and enjoyed their parks and gardens. The walks in this book aim to integrate these various facets of West London's history. By the time the walker has followed them all, he or she will have walked the Thames from Putney to Windsor and will have seen much of the surrounding watershed, rivers and canals and visited most of the larger parks and open spaces. Walks 1 to 9 are centred on the Thames towpath; the remainder on parks, tributaries of the Thames, and the Grand Union Canal. They are all on the Ordnance Survey map of West London, sheet number 176.

It should be borne in mind that while specific permission to walk the towpaths is not normally required, they do not necessarily constitute public rights of way, and consequently the public walk them at their own risk. It must also be remembered that towpaths can sometimes be very muddy.

Buses and trains serving the area are normally reasonably frequent and reliable, but it is always advisable to check local timetables.

WRAYSBURY — RUNNYMEDE — RIVER THAMES — DATCHET

7 miles

This is not a circular walk; return by train to Wraysbury Station — reasonably frequent trains, but timetable at station should be noted.

This walk leaves Wraysbury Station and passes between Wraysbury Reservoir and gravel pits to reach the river Thames. A long walk along the banks of the Thames through Runnymede is followed by a half mile stretch of road to Datchet and a short train ride back to Wraysbury Station.

How to get there: By car — leave the M4 at junction 5 to Colnbrook, Horton and then Wraysbury. Parking is available at Wraysbury Station. By train — British Rail from Waterloo to Wraysbury Station.

Leave Wraysbury Station car park and bear right along the road. After 25 yards, just over the bridge, leave the road to the right, taking a small path across a stream. Walk along the left-hand bank of the river Colne to meet the railway line after 100 yards. Follow the line on its left-hand side along a narrow path almost overgrown in places, for about a quarter of a mile. Cross the railway line to the right at the first crossing place.

Directly ahead, across rough ground, there is a bridge over Colne Brook which is flowing to the left to meet the Thames. Follow this river to the left. Do not confuse the river with one of the gravel pits, which contain only static water. The paths on either side of the river are well used by anglers but are in need of attention in places. Follow the sometimes muddy way between bullrushes, nettles, trees and bushes. After approximately a quarter of a mile bear to the left, following the water, and proceed for about the same distance again. Cross the flowing river to the right by the walkway to emerge after approximately 50 yards at Hythe End. Here turn right along the road.

Cross the single-lane road bridge and after 50 yards, where four roads meet, turn to the left, almost backtracking, down Ferry Lane. Pass along the backs of private houses, taking the left-hand fork where the track branches. (The right-hand branch is a private road.) Entering a group of small factories, take an alleyway to the left between two sections of a factory. At the back of the factory cross the fast-running river at the weir and walk directly ahead, emerging on to the A30 road.

Turn right and follow the main road round without crossing. Cross the Thames at Runnymede Bridge and immediately descend to the right to join the river by Bellwell Lock. Walk upstream, past the restaurant, lock and boatyard following the towpath. After half a mile you arrive at the open meadow where King John is thought to have put his seal to the first copy of Magna Carta. The Barons had marched from London and crossed the river at Staines. Having established themselves in the meadows, they negotiated with King John for several days before he came down from Windsor to meet them. The exact spot of the signing is a matter for debate; it may have been in the meadows or on Magna Carta Island itself.

Follow the curve in the river, or cut across the meadow, passing Magna Carta Island opposite. On this bank of the river pass the Magna Carta Memorial and that to John F. Kennedy, set in three acres of land given to the United States. Continue along the riverside, past a refreshment hut, for about a mile to where the road runs close to boatyards. Continue along the backs of houses and cross a footbridge to the right to continue along the bank of the main river.

Pass Old Windsor Lock, the road bridge on to Ham Fields and then the weir. At Albert Bridge the river path is blocked by an iron gate. This area is within the grounds of Windsor Castle and is not open to the public. Cross the Thames at Albert Bridge and follow the B3021 into Datchet (about half a mile). In Datchet turn right to the station, signposted *Car Parking*.

There are frequent trains back to Wraysbury Station from here — about two an hour at weekends.

LALEHAM — STAINES — RUNNYMEDE — EGHAM — THORPE — ABBEY MEADE — CHERTSEY — LALEHAM

11 miles

Although a casual glance at the Ordnance Survey map might suggest that much of the riverside from Laleham to Runnymede is built up, this is not so and there is good rural walking all the way. Starting opposite Laleham Burway, the walk follows the left bank of the Thames upstream past Penton Hook, now a vast boating marina. It then passes along the rear of some most attractive houses and up into Staines. Here, after crossing the bridge, it takes the right-hand bank up to Runnymede and then follows the A30 across Runnymede Fields. After a short walk through Egham, the route crosses by Milton Park to Thorpe village. Monk's Walk then leads through Thorpe Water Park and Leisure Centre back to Chertsey and it is only a short walk upstream back to the car.

How to get there: By train — British Rail from Waterloo to Chertsey, and then by bus No. 459 from Chertsey Station to Chertsey Bridge. Cross Chertsey Bridge and then turn sharp left in front of the Chertsey Lock Club and Restaurant. Pass the lock and the weir and walk along the river bank for 400 yards to the car park at the recreation ground. By bus — No. 459 from Feltham via Shepperton and Sunbury to Chertsey Bridge, then follow above directions to the recreation ground. By car — Parking is available at the recreation ground, half way between Chertsey Lock and Laleham alongside the Thames.

Leave the car park at the recreation ground and head up-river with the river bank on your left. After 150 yards pass the raised grassy banks of Laleham Burway on the opposite bank and carry on round the gentle bend in the river for 300 yards.

At the sharp bend in the road, carry straight on where the sign 'No through road' appears in front of some attractive houses. At the wooden barrier, 200 yards further on, follow the bank of the river marked 'Public Footpath — Staines 2¼ miles'. Pass the Thames Water Authority inlet on your right. From here water is pumped up to the Queen Mary reservoir. Head for the weir mouth now visible ahead and after 300 yards pass Penton Hook Lock and weirs. The large marina lies around the bend in the river away to the left and as such is not visible.

Follow the river bank for half a mile, to where a grassy area opens out and the river curves around ninety degrees to the right. A metalled path leads along 'Thameside' past the church of St. Peter and then past a brick shelter to where the rail bridge crosses the river.

Immediately after the rail bridge, take the road passing forward and slightly to the right, keeping to the left-hand side past the *Pack Horse* Hotel to reach the traffic lights after 200 yards. Here turn left to Staines Bridge, heading in the direction of the gas-holder. Pass the Town Hall and public conveniences on your left and then the cinema and restaurant. Turn left over the river and on the opposite bank take the steps down to the riverside.

Follow the river upstream, under Staines Bridge, passing in turn a boatyard, culvert, engineering works and gas-holders. Pass the water inlet and then cross a footbridge over a small inlet to reach Runnymede Bridge. Pass under Runnymede Bridge and turn up to the left immediately afterwards, following the A30 towards Windsor. At the large roundabout, cross the A308 with care to follow the A30 signposted towards Southampton and Basingstoke.

Follow the path in Runnymede Fields to the right of the main road for a quarter of a mile; then bear to the left to meet the road approximately 300 yards from a roundabout. Cross the A30 and take the narrow Langham Place, by a small row of cottages, to the left. At the end of Langham Place, after 100 yards, turn left opposite Runnymede Galleries. After 50 yards, having passed the Salvation Army Hall and a garage, turn right into Limes Road and follow this round to the right. At the end of Limes Road do not enter The Crescent, but turn left into North Street. Pass a coalyard on the right and the *Foresters' Arms*, and cross Rusham Road to take the footbridge over the railway line.

Turn right immediately on the far side. With the railway on your right, walk for 100 yards with allotments on your left. Bear away from the railway line to the left and walk between fences for 300 yards. At the end of the fences pass a house on the right and cross the stile to emerge on a short lane with the B.P. Research Laboratories on your left.

After 75 yards, at the end of the lane, turn left into Prune Hill. With the automatic crossing gates behind you, walk for 200 yards to where the road turns sharply to the left. Here, turn right into Whitehall Farm and immediately take the public footpath marked to the left, crossing a stile after 50 yards.

Note the sanatorium on the hill to the right and Royal Holloway College behind you. Make for the far right-hand corner of this large field and here cross the stream by the wooden bridge, passing forward between fences with arable land on both sides. After 250 yards cross the metalled road slightly to the left to take the public footpath marked to Thorpe. Note the impressive Manor House of Great Fosters. Traverse the left-hand side of this field, with arable land on the left giving way to a small plantation of conifers at the bottom. Enter the narrow strip of woodland directly ahead and cross the wide bridge over the M25. From here it is possible to get a good view over Thorpe and Egham.

After crossing this bridge, walk forward and to the right to cross a stile on to the metalled road. Cross this and in 20 yards take the initially metalled lane to the left, which soon becomes more rugged. After 75 yards, at the left-hand side of the first house, take the public footpath left for 300 yards between fences. At Thorpe Stores, turn right and follow the road round to the left and then right again. At the *Red Lion* public house turn left into Coldharbour Lane and follow the brick wall on the right to its end after 250 yards. On reaching Church Approach, cross the stone stile directly ahead to take the public footpath marked to Chertsey.

For three-quarters of a mile walk directly ahead on Monk's Way, along which the monks from Chertsey Abbey used to pass. On your right are the intricate inlets and islets of Thorpe Water Park and its competition lake. To your left is the new Thorpe Leisure Centre. At the far end of the track cross the bridge over the connecting waterway and then cross a stile towards the motorway. Pass under the A320 and then zig-zag up its far side to cross the M3 by the bridge. From this vantage point note the church tower in the direction of Chertsey, for which we are heading. Zig-zag down to the left on the far side of the motorway and take the first road to the left towards the church tower. On your immediate left are fields and the motorway.

Walk down the road for 300 yards to public conveniences at the corner of a playing field. Cross to the far corner of the field and then turn left along the road towards the site of the old abbey with modern houses on your right. At Abbey Green turn right and after 25 yards, at the bottom, take the bridleway to the left down Willow Walk by Manor Farm Cottages. Bearing right and then left, carry straight ahead to emerge on the B375 after 150 yards. Turn left and then bear round with the road to the right towards Shepperton for 400 yards. Cross the traffic lights and pass the *Cricketers* and the *Galleon* public houses to Chertsey Bridge.

To return to the recreation ground, cross Chertsey Bridge and then turn sharp left in front of the Chertsey Lock Club and Restaurant. Pass the lock and the weir and walk along the river bank for 400 yards to where you parked the car.

Walk 3

WALTON-ON-THAMES — RIVER THAMES TO RIVER WEY — CHERTSEY — SHEPPERTON — WALTON-ON-THAMES

7½ miles or 2 miles

This is an extremely attractive walk, starting along a part of the Thames favoured by anglers and the boating fraternity. At Weybridge the Thames is joined by the rivers Wey and Bourne and the route follows the Wey for a mile before cutting back across country to rejoin the Thames at Chertsey Bridge. From here there are two alternative routes:

(1)   This passes by the flooded gravel pits at Littleton, which are used for angling and sailing. Waterfowl such as teal, grebe, coot, mallard and heron can often be seen on the water, together with divers and migratory seabirds in the winter months. Then the route rejoins the river and it is a short road walk back into Walton.

(2)   This route may involve slightly more road walking unless the ferry at Shepperton Lock is in operation. This can be ascertained during the first part of the walk up the opposite bank. From Chertsey Bridge the ferry follows the Thames back down to Dockett Point and Shepperton Lock. If the ferry is not in operation then the road is followed back into Walton. The ferry will take you to the opposite bank and you then follow the line of the Desborough Cut back to the car park.

A very short route of 2 miles is also included; this is a circular walk around the Halliford Bend.

How to get there: By car — parking available at Walton-on-Thames Bridge. By train — British Rail from Waterloo to Walton-on-Thames Station, and then No. 218 bus from main road outside station to Walton Bridge.

From the car park at Walton Bridge, head upstream with the river on your right. After 400 yards you will come to a concrete and wood bridge beyond which is the Desborough Cut, opened in 1935 to cut out the long Halliford Bend to

15

Shepperton, and named after the then Chairman of the Thames Conservancy Board. Cross this bridge to the other bank of the canal to follow the curve of the main river round to the right. Pass waterworks on your left and follow the metalled track signposted in the direction of the Vandals' Rugby Football and Cricket Ground (Brownacres), until it peters out. Here, carry straight on with the river on your right around this great bend for about three-quarters of a mile. On the opposite bank are large houses and later a road with several hotels. As the road on the opposite bank veers away, a sailing centre and then open fields and gravel pits come into view. Follow the path to the far end of the Desborough Cut.

For the short, two-mile walk, turn left when you reach the far end of the Desborough Cut and follow this back to the car park.

To continue with the longer walk, when you reach the far end of the Desborough Cut, cross the bridge and turn upstream to your right. You will soon come upon Eyot House on an island in the middle of the river. A narrow footbridge joins the island to the bank. Shepperton Lock is now visible on the opposite bank with a second island beyond. Note whether or not the ferry is in operation from the island, since this may influence your choice of route for the return journey.

The reason why the river channels appear so complicated at this point is partly because the rivers Wey and Bourne, together with the Wey Navigation Canal, here enter the Thames from the left. The many streams of water and small islands create considerable confusion in midstream, with the main Thames passage for boats along the far bank of the river, behind the weir. Originally, the Wey was an important route to the Wey and Arun Canal, which in turn led to the river Arun and the south coast, but this canal has been closed for more than 100 years. The river Wey is, however, still navigable as far as Guildford and sometimes as far as Godalming.

The riverside path veers left along a wooden fence and after passing through a small car park joins the road uphill for a short distance. Walk uphill past the *Lincoln Arms* on the left-hand side of the road for 100 yards until you reach the *Old*

Crown Inn. Take the pedestrian alleyway past public conveniences on this side of the pub at the far end of the car park.

Cross the first small road after 25 yards, passing a row of six cottages on your left, and cross the next road into Church Walk. Turn right immediately after the row of cottages on the right, and cross the footbridge. Cross the metalled road to enter a narrow alleyway between wire mesh and corrugated iron fencing. Follow the concrete path for 100 yards before climbing over the wooden bridge at Thames Lock, where boats on the river Wey enter the Thames. Here, turn to the left, following the path, and entering National Trust land, walk up this side of the river with the water on your left for about half a mile. On the opposite bank are large houses with their gardens coming down to the river. Shortly, to your right, a metalled road will become visible through the trees. This is the road for which we are heading, albeit by a roundabout route. Follow the river to the first of two large road bridges and climb the bank on to the first bridge. This carries the A317 road, which we follow for about 50 yards in the direction of Chertsey; at this point a public footpath is signposted to Ham Court (cul-de-sac). Take this metalled track for 300 yards to a Y-fork.

Turn left and follow the public footpath over fields in the direction of pylons supporting power cables. Cross a stile after 100 yards, then an isolated broken gate, and pass under the electricity cables to the far side of the field. At the caravan site, turn right and follow the line of pylons over a further stile. Follow the track until you come upon an old road, leading from derelict farm buildings. Turn left for 100 yards to the edge of the woods in Woburn Park. Turn right along the well-worn track and cross the river directly ahead after 250 yards.

Turn immediately left along the bank of the river, following a single line of pylons, but slowly veer away from the river to your right, crossing the arable land to meet a metalled track towards Chertsey. This runs about 300 yards away from the edge of the woods. Having met this road, follow it to the left through Chertsey Mead. Two other roads leave it to the right towards private houses, but disregard them. Turn right immediately after the boatyard between tall wire mesh fences.

After 150 yards, at the end of the fences turn left and pass through a small factory estate to emerge at Chertsey Bridge after 200 yards.

Cross the bridge and turn right along the marked public footpath by the side of the river. Follow the curve of the river to the left for 400 yards to a small iron kissing-gate.

Here, you should decide whether to return via Littleton gravel pits (1) or follow the river to Shepperton (2).

(1) *Via Littleton Gravel Pits:*
Do not pass through the kissing-gate but veer further to the left alongside the hedge for 50 yards, back towards the road. Climb over the wooden stile and cross the road slightly to the right, into Littleton Lane, signposted to Laleham and Staines. Follow this road for 200 yards. Immediately after crossing the motorway take the public footpath signposted to the right and zig-zag down the grassy bank. Follow this path along the side of the motorway, with the moored yachts of Littleton Sailing Club on the water to your immediate left.

After 150 yards, veer to the left away from the motorway along a narrow strip of land between the two man-made lakes, perhaps stopping to admire the waterfowl. After 250 yards, just before the path rises onto a dilapidated concrete foot-bridge, take the right-hand fork in the path, again between two lakes. Follow the right-hand path from the fork as it weaves its way between the water, following a line of dead elms first to the left and then to the right. After about 400 yards, cross the small concrete weir to your left, and passing straight forward, emerge onto a small cul-de-sac. Turn right and cross the main road after 25 yards, onto the footpath directly opposite, heading towards the footbridge visible directly ahead.

Cross this footbridge over the motorway and, after enjoying the view, carry straight ahead between fields and common land to where the path reaches the rear of an infant school and private houses. Emerge onto School Lane, a short road, and turn right into the High Street at the *Three Horseshoes* public house. After 25 yards, at the Green, turn left into Russell Road and follow this round to the left to the *River View Hotel*.

Here, turn right into Walton Lane, following the curve in

the river (Halliford Bend). Ignore side turnings and follow through the one-way section to emerge shortly at Walton Bridge. Cross either of the bridges and turn right immediately, to the car park where the walk started.

(2) *From Chertsey Bridge back along the river:*
Pass through the iron kissing-gate and follow the bank of the river past moored houseboats and small launches. After half a mile meet and continue along the metalled Ferry Lane, keeping to the grass verges. Follow the road to Shepperton Lock with its public conveniences.

If the ferry is in operation then you may take it to the opposite bank and follow the river in the direction from which we initially came, this time following the line of the Desborough Cut instead of the Halliford Bend. If the ferry is not operating (as is usually the case), then continue around the road, which turns sharp left, past the Ship's Chandlers and boatyard. After 400 yards meet the B375 road and turn right.

There is now about one mile of pleasant road walking back to Walton Bridge. Follow the road to the left at St. Nicholas' church and continue until the Green opens out on your right. Ignore the High Street to the left, but bear right and follow the main road to the *River View Hotel.*

At the *River View Hotel,* turn right into Walton Lane, following the curve in the river (Halliford Bend). Ignore side turnings and follow through the one-way section to emerge at Walton Bridge. Cross either of the bridges and turn right immediately, to the car park where the walk started.

WALTON-ON-THAMES — RIVER THAMES TO HAMPTON COURT — WEST MOLESEY — RIVER MOLE — RIVER EMBER — BEESBOROUGH AND KNIGHT RESERVOIRS — WALTON-ON-THAMES

11 miles

The walk starts at Walton Bridge and follows the Thames downstream. A large part of the riverside in this area adjoins reservoirs and these are much in evidence during most of this section. On reaching Hampton Court we leave the Thames and after half a mile reach the river Ember, which is followed through common land around Island Barn Reservoir. After passing Beesborough and Knight Reservoirs, the walk returns to the bank of the Thames close by the central waterworks for the area. Turning back at Sunbury Lock, it follows the Thames back into Walton.

How to get there: By car — parking is available by Walton-on-Thames Bridge. By train — British Rail from Waterloo to Walton-on-Thames Station, then bus No. 218 from the station to Walton Bridge. Alternatively, by train from Waterloo to Hampton Court Station and join the walk at Hampton Court.

Leaving the car park just upstream of Walton Bridge, follow the river downstream under the bridge itself. Pass in front of the Marine Stores and Chandler's Shop and cross the foot-bridge. Continue along the towpath below large houses for one third of a mile to *The Swan* and *The Anglers* public houses, almost opposite the first weir. Continue past the pubs, and then pass a small park and Walton Rowing Club on your right after half a mile.

After a third of a mile, pass a second weir on the opposite bank and the oil terminal on the near side of the river. Follow the towpath with the road to your right slightly above you, to arrive at the new Elmbridge Leisure Centre and then another public house on the right. To your left water tumbles over a large weir. Follow the canalised branch of the river to Sunbury

Locks (Sunbury New Lock was opened by Lord Desborough of Taplow in 1927; the same Lord Desborough gives his name to the Desborough Cut above Walton Bridge).

About 150 yards downstream from the locks, on the right, just at the boundary of the Thames Water Authority's land, a narrow path enters along the fence. **Do not take this path**, but note that this is where we shall rejoin the river on the return journey. Continue along the towpath for a further mile below the Molesey Reservoirs. Note Sunbury Court on the opposite bank — an imposing Georgian-style building used by the Salvation Army as a recreation centre. After leaving the reservoirs, the path emerges along the rear of private houses. Garrick's Temple, built as a folly by the actor of that name, is visible on the opposite bank shortly before Platt's Eyot, a large island used for boatyards and the home of Thornycroft's, a firm famous for torpedo boats in both World Wars.

The riverside now opens out to a grassy field behind modern developments and the path follows the river, first along a disused road and then flanked by tall trees. Pass the open-air swimming pool to reach Molesey Lock close by Hampton Court Bridge. Molesey Lock is the highest point on the river that fish can reach. Emerge at Riverside; the road goes forward towards Hampton Court. After 100 yards turn right where the *Thames Hotel* stands on the corner.

Walk up the narrow street, full of antique shops and cafés. After 100 yards, at the end, bear right up Creek Road and follow this to the left, ignoring side turnings, until it becomes Bridge Road after about 200 yards. Pass a public house on the left and then turn sharp right at a bend into Walton Road (B369) and head towards the distant church spire. Take the second turning on the left, 200 yards along Walton Road; you will soon come upon the parish church of St. Mary. Here turn right into St. Mary's Road and follow this to the left past the *Bell Inn*; keep to the left-hand fork in the road into Bell Road.

After 100 yards, by the entrance to East Molesey Court at the end of Bell Road, turn sharp left down a gravel alleyway with fences on both sides; after 100 yards cross the concrete bridge. Bear right, following the fences with the river on your left. After 200 yards the ground opens out with grass to your right. Follow the fence on the right-hand side and take the track to the right towards the raised grass sides of Island Barn Reservoir, which is clearly visible. The dirt track leads onto a narrow concrete path as it heads towards the towers, and the steps cut into the sides of the reservoir. The path then bends to the right around playing fields and to the front of the reservoir, following the fences. Pass the remnants of a wooden gate and carry straight on to meet the river again after about 150 yards.

At the weir, turn left upstream and follow the track onto playing fields. Pass a metalled bridge from the estate on the right and carry straight on with the river on your right-hand side. At the far side of the playing field, pass concrete posts onto a narrow path between bushes and a fence.

After 200 yards you will come to the bridge from Island Barn Reservoir and the Sailing Club. Here, cross to the other bank of the river Mole and continue upstream on the right-hand side. After another 100 yards, pass more concrete posts and allotments on the right. Follow the river as it bends and cross straight over the road at the next brick bridge to continue along the riverside path at the back of a new housing development. Ignore the small bridge to the left 200 yards further on, and carry straight ahead towards Queen Elizabeth II Reservoir, the grassy banks of which can now be seen. Emerge shortly onto the Molesey Road and turn right.

Walk along Molesey Road for 300 yards until you reach the end of Queen Elizabeth II Reservoir, and then turn left along the B369 (Walton Road) with Queen Elizabeth II Reservoir on your left and Beesborough Reservoir on your right. Keep to the verge of this road, and after half a mile bear to the right, with Knight Reservoir on your left, to meet the A3050.

At the T-junction, turn right along Hurst Road, with Knight Reservoir on your right. Walk for 300 yards, past App's Court Farm, to the boundary fence of the waterworks. Here, on the left-hand side of the road, take the narrow signposted public footpath between fences, back down towards the river, with farmland on your left and the tanks of the waterworks on your immediate right. After 300 yards, emerge on the river bank just below Sunbury Locks. Turn left and climb up to the locks themselves. Pass these, and keep along this side of the river, past the Leisure Centre and oil terminal, and follow the river bank back into Walton-on-Thames, where we left the car.

BUSHEY PARK — WOODLAND GARDENS — HAMPTON COURT — KINGSTON BRIDGE — BUSHEY PARK

6 miles, 4 miles, or 5 miles

Starting in the Royal Park, the walk proceeds through the semi-formal Woodland Gardens and then through open parkland to Hampton Court. In the deer park behind the palace itself, deer are always to be seen. From Hampton Court there is a choice of three routes:
(1) Along the riverside
(2) A short route through the gardens of the palace and deer park
(3) A longer route through the palace gardens and deer park.

From the back of Hampton Court Deer Park, the walk re-enters the rear of Bushey Park at Kingston Bridge. Deer are also to be found throughout the year in Bushey Park.

How to get there: By car — Enter Bushey Park at the Teddington Gate close to the National Physical Laboratory. Take the first road to the right inside the gate and park at the first car park on the left. By train — British Rail from Waterloo to Hampton Court Station. Cross the bridge and commence the walk at (1). By boat — From Westminster Pier (takes 4 hours).

From the car park, standing with your back to the Queen's House on the other side of the road, strike off across open ground, slightly to the left towards the wooden fence 300 yards away at the boundary of the Woodland Gardens. Enter the Woodland Gardens by the wooden gate. Walk forward over the wooden bridge and turn to the right alongside the lake. Follow the path through rhododendrons and azaleas, past the Warden's Cottage with the small culvert on your right. Leave the first part of the gardens at the gate and cross a grassy ride directly to enter the second part through another gate.

The waterways and lakes in Bushey and Hampton Court Park are fed by the Duke of Northumberland's Longford

River, an artificial waterway created by Charles I to provide drinking water for his deer. It flows across Hounslow Heath from the river Colne and has a branch to Syon Park.

Walk forward, past the tunnelled path which enters from the left, and after 75 yards follow the main path round to the left. At a T-junction, turn left passing a miniature weir and cross the wooden bridge to the right. Keep to the right of the pond and, veering slightly to the right, proceed through bushes to meet a larger lake. Follow the outflow from this lake to the left, and after 100 yards leave the gardens by the gate. Directly ahead, on the other side of the road, is the Thames.

Do not leave the park but turn left along the path. After 300 yards veer to the right to reach the back of a tall brick wall. Follow along, with this wall on your right-hand side, behind a large Regency-style house and later the shells of empty buildings. Deer are often to be found grazing in this part of the park. After another 400 yards, leave the park to the right by the road which comes from the Diana Fountain.

Cross the main road at the pedestrian crossing and enter Hampton Court through the gates directly ahead. Take the path to the right signposted 'Restaurant, Car Park and State Apartments'. After 100 yards veer to the left between brick walls and under an archway to reach the front of Hampton Court Palace. You should now decide which route you wish to follow.

(1) *Along the riverside:*
Do not enter the Palace, but turn right down the wide drive to the Trophy Gates. Pass through these, and immediately turn left towards Hampton Court Bridge. Do not cross the river, but turn left along the towpath with the water on your right-hand side. On the left is the brick wall of the palace and shortly after, the Tijou Screen of wrought iron.

Continue along the path and on your left the back gardens of the palace come into view. On your right are pleasure-cruise jetties and, across the river, moorings for private boats and houseboats. Pass the Pavilion on your left (now a private house) with views across the open deer park and golf course. For a short way the towpath is paved with cobble-stones.

The path passes through blackthorn bushes and banks of wild flowers, and is a favourite spot for anglers. As you round the left-hand bend in the river, the twin chimneys of Kingston 'B' Power Station can be seen in the distance. Pass Raven's Ait, a man-made island in the middle of the river used as a sailing centre.

At Kingston Bridge(*), bear to the left to the main road, with open ground beyond railings on your left. Turn to the left and, crossing by one of the zebra crossings, enter Church Grove opposite (**). After 75 yards, at the parish church of St. John the Baptist, pass through the iron gates in the left-hand wall, opposite the church itself. Enter upon an avenue of sweet chestnuts, with a children's playground on the left and allotments on the right. At the other end leave by more gates to re-enter Bushey Park.

Walk across the open ground to the right, towards the nearest copse at its right-hand corner. Rounding this copse, cross the water at the bridge and carry straight on uphill, first crossing a well-marked dirt track and later a tarred track which leads left to a keeper's cottage. After crossing this tarred track, veer round slightly left to a coppice of young trees protected against deer by wooden fences. Pass this and then cross a grassy ride of sweet chestnuts to meet the main metalled road through the park. Cross this directly and follow the road opposite back to the car park.

(2) *Through the Palace and Deer Park by the short route:*
Hampton Court was extensively modified in 1514 by the ambitious Cardinal Wolsey; it was later taken over by Henry VIII when Wolsey fell from favour. Henry lived there with five of his six wives and during this time he stocked the park with deer. It was here that he played Royal Tennis and enjoyed jousting in the Tiltyard Gardens. The State Apartments are worth visiting, as are the kitchens, bed-chambers and guard-room. Of special note are the tapestries and Renaissance ceilings. Outside, Anne Boleyn's Gateway, the Astronomical Clock, maze, orangery, great vine, wilderness, sunken garden and knot garden are kept impeccably. When Wolsey modified the palace, the river water was drinkable at this point. Wolsey, however, distrusted its purity and arranged for spring water to

be brought by a double lead pipeline from Coombe Hill, three and a half miles away above Kingston.

During the summer the back gates of the deer park are closed at 8.30 p.m. During the winter they are closed at 6 p.m. every day except Sunday, when they close at 5 p.m.

Enter the Palace through the front arch. If you wish to look inside the Palace you should do so at this stage. Otherwise, pass through Base Court, Clock Court (with the famous astronomical clock showing seasons, phases of the moon, etc.), and Fountain Court, to emerge at the back of the Palace.

With your back to the Palace you will see four paths in front of you. Take the second on the left, leading in the direction of Stud House. After 150 yards, cross the footbridge and go through the iron gates. Follow the broad ride with lime trees on both sides. This part of the park abounds with deer which are fascinating to watch. During the rutting season (September to October) or when the hinds have young fawns, they should not be approached too closely.

Cross directly over the track from Stud House. Continue straight ahead and after about half a mile go uphill past a small pond on the left to meet a metalled road. Follow this road to the left, to leave Hampton Court by the Kingston Gate. Cross the main road to enter Church Grove opposite. Continue with directions given in (1) from the double asterisk (**) to the end of the walk.

(3) *Longer route through the Palace and Deer Park:*
Entering the Palace through the front arch, pass through Base, Clock and Fountain Courts to emerge at the rear of the Palace. From the rear of the Palace, take the second path on your right. After 150 yards cross the water by the bridge and enter the deer park via the iron gate. Follow the broad ride directly ahead but **do not** take the gravel path to the left. With the golf course on your right, pass the club-house after 600 yards.

Turn left at the wooden fence beyond and follow this fence for about 300 yards. At the boating lake on the left, turn right through an iron gate and walk down a fenced area to reach the river after 100 yards. Turn left at Raven's Ait and follow the towpath for 600 yards to Kingston Bridge. Continue the walk by following the route given from this point (*) in (1).

HAM HOUSE — RIVER THAMES TO TEDDINGTON LOCK AND KINGSTON — RICHMOND PARK — HAM HOUSE

6 miles or 6½ miles

This is a delightful walk. It combines river-bank walking with views over the river from the high ground of Richmond Park. From Ham House the route passes upstream past Teddington Lock along the Thames to Kingston-on-Thames. From just below Kingston Bridge it involves walking for about half a mile through interesting Victorian streets before it enters Richmond Park at the Kingston Gate. After walking through the park there is then a choice of two routes:
(1) Leaving by the Ham Gate, across Ham Common and back to Ham House.
(2) A slightly longer route via the Star and Garter Gate at the top of Richmond Hill, across Petersham Common and Fields and along the river-bank back to Ham House.

How to get there: By car — parking available outside Ham House entrance. By rail — British Rail from Waterloo to Richmond Station; then by bus No. 71 to Ham House.

Ham House is a beautiful seventeenth-century brick mansion, now owned by the National Trust. Originally built as a manor house, it became the property of the Duke and Duchess of Lauderdale in the late seventeenth century, and was completely redecorated in the style of the period. Today it survives in almost its original state with a profusion of rich hangings, parquetry floors, plaster ceilings and chimney-pieces. There is much interesting furniture of the period together with Delft tulip vases and K'ang-Hsi porcelain. When the house was improved in 1637 the magnificent staircase was added. The whole house and its contents are evocative of the period, and the house and its extensive grounds are open throughout the year.

Leaving the car in Ham House car park by the riverside,

take the towpath upstream with the Thames on your right-hand side and common ground on your left. On the far side of the common ground is Richmond Small Arms Club, whose firing you may be able to hear. After approximately 200 yards pass Eel Pie Island on the far side of the river; its name denotes a local delicacy of a bygone era. After half a mile rise slightly past lock gates which allow water and boats into a private yacht basin called Ham Dock, once a gravel pit.

Cross the bridge over the lock entrance and follow the towpath upstream among trees and shrubs. About 100 yards further on, surrounded by an iron fence on the right-hand side of the path and partly hidden by bushes, is a stone monument. This was erected in 1909 and marks the river boundary between the Thames Conservancy Board's lower limit and the Port of London's landward limit when the latter was formed in that year. Continue along the side of the river with views of many beautiful houses on the opposite bank, to arrive at Teddington Lock and weir. There is an attractive public house on the opposite bank, reached by a series of gantries.

The first weir here was built in 1812 and reconstructed several times; the present reconstruction was completed in 1950. The amount of water flowing over the weir is gauged daily as an indication of the volume flowing in the river as a whole. This amount, plus that taken by the Thames Water Authority, varies from approximately 400 million gallons per day in summer to approximately 1500 million gallons per day in a major flood. There are three locks at Teddington. The Barge Lock is the largest on the river. The Launch Lock is the original one, and the Skiff Lock is the smallest, being known affectionately as 'the coffin' on account of its size and shape. Because the Thames is tidal as far as Teddington, the weir is raised and lowered at high and low tide to maintain the water level in the river above this point. Because of this, the maximum rise and fall in water levels ever recorded above Teddington was just over ten feet.

Continuing along the bank of the river, another mile or so of walking will bring you on to a metalled road opposite Kingston Sailing Club. Follow this road, with large houses above and to your left, for about 250 yards, where it starts to veer away from the river. Here, take the wide gravel road to the right which starts just beyond the wooden barrier. Following the river closely, pass the boat-houses, café and tennis courts on your left and then turn left up a narrow alleyway of sweet chestnuts just after public conveniences. Kingston 'B' Power Station is on your immediate right-hand side.

At the end of the alleyway, pass forward and slightly to the left, up King's Road. On high ground approximately half a mile ahead the tall trees in Richmond Park can be seen. Carry on up King's Road, crossing the Richmond Road at a cross-roads and walking straight on up the road as it climbs towards Richmond Park. The houses on this road are typical of the late eighteenth-century cottages built on the periphery of London, and are mostly in a good state of repair. Pass the 'Keep' (a new housing development) and the Catholic church and carry on straight up the hill, bearing slightly to the right. After another 250 yards you come suddenly upon the Kingston Gate of Richmond Park at a T-junction. Turn left into the park.

Study the map of the park just inside the gate on the left and head in the direction of the Ham Gate. Follow the road initially past the public conveniences, but then branch from it to the left to descend through oaks and other deciduous trees, with a high brick wall to your left. Descend to meet the metalled road which leaves the park at Ham Gate to the left.

(1) *Short route back across Ham Common:*
Turn left with the small pond on your right and leave the park through the Ham Gate. Pass a large house on the left and a road entering from the left. Carry straight on through the woods to the left of the road, taking any one of the many tracks. After 400 yards pass two open areas on the left, which are used as horse-training rings. To your left, through the trees, it may be possible to see the twin spires of a church. Meeting the main Richmond Road, carry straight across to a triangle of open grassland with Regency houses on the left and larger ones on the right.

Veer to your right across this small part of Ham Common to meet the metalled road. Follow this left, past St. Michael's Convent of the 'Sisters of the Church', and turn right just after Avenue Lodge through white gates and fencing which open onto a wide horse ride. To the front is Ham House.

Follow the ride forward across a metalled road and through
more white gates to the wrought-iron gates at the back of Ham
House. If these are open, then it is possible to walk through the
grounds to emerge at the front of the house. If not, then follow
the wall along to the right, turning left at the end. Proceed with
the polo field on your right and the brick wall on your left, to
the end of the wall where you turn left along the front of the
house itself. Turn right at the metalled road to return to the car
park where the walk started.

(2) *Longer route via Star and Garter Gate:*
Cross the metalled road with the small pond on your left-hand
side. Follow the winding track uphill slightly to the right. From
the top of the hill there is a magnificent view over Ham and
Kingston and it is possible to trace the route followed so far.
Continue forward and slightly right to meet the metalled road
and pass Pembroke Lodge on your left. Pembroke Lodge was
built in the mid-eighteenth century on the site of an old
mole-catcher's cottage. It was originally a 'grace and favour'
residence. George III lent it to the Countess of Pembroke until
her death in 1831 and Queen Victoria let Lord John Russell,
one of her Prime Ministers, live there. It is now a restaurant.
  Follow the road past the car park to the Star and Garter
Gate on the left. Leave the park and turn down the hill to the
left, crossing the road after 25 yards to enter Petersham
Common on the right just behind the Star and Garter Disabled Servicemen's Home. Cross the common, traversing to
the right, downhill, to meet the Richmond Road at the foot of
the hill. Turn right and follow this road towards Richmond,
crossing it at the Tudor Close Restaurant. About one hundred
yards further on, on the left-hand side of the road, a path
enters Petersham Meadows just before public conveniences.
Walk ahead towards the river with the open Petersham
Meadows to your left, on which cattle often graze, and the
Riverside Park of the Terraced Gardens on your right. At the
river, bear left, following it back upstream to Ham House just
over half a mile away.

KEW — RIVER THAMES TO RICHMOND — RICHMOND PARK — EAST SHEEN — BARNES — RIVER THAMES TO KEW

7½ miles

Starting by Kew Gardens, the Thames towpath is followed upstream to Richmond. Then the route climbs to the higher ground of Richmond Park at the Star and Garter Gate, and crosses the northern side of the park to leave by the Roehampton Gate near the Beverley Brook. A short walk through the streets of East Sheen and Mortlake leads down to the Thames again at Barnes and then back upstream to Kew.

How to get there: By car — parking is available outside the entrance to Kew Gardens or in the car park by the river in Ferry Road. By train — British Rail (a) Waterloo to Kew Bridge, (b) Broad Street to Kew Gardens. By underground — District Line to Kew Gardens. By bus — No. 117 Shepherd's Bush to Staines; No. 267 Hammersmith to Hampton Court; No. 27 Highgate to Teddington or Richmond; No. 65 Ealing to Chessington Zoo; No. 15 East Ham to Kew Gardens (summer Sundays only) — alight at Kew Bridge.

In or around 1759, Augusta, mother of George II, planted 9 acres of trees at Kew. These gardens were expanded by successive monarchs in the 18th and 19th centuries until they were acquired by the state in 1841. They have two parts: a western arboretum and eastern formal lawns and gardens. There are tropical and temperate glass-houses including Decimus Burton's famous Palm House of glass and wrought-iron, built between 1844 and 1848. In the gardens are several interesting items: a Japanese octagonal pagoda, a 225-foot flagpole from British Columbia, an oriental gateway, and four temples. Queen Charlotte's Cottage in the arboretum was built in 1772 and has an internal decor designed to give one the impression of being in a tent. The gardens and houses are open to the public daily.

Leaving the car park by the riverside at Kew, follow the towpath upstream with the gardens on your left and the river Thames and Brentford Ait on the opposite bank. After about one mile, look out for Syon House across the river. After Kew Gardens, pass Richmond Golf Course on the left and at a bend in the river, Twickenham Ait opposite, just after the *London Apprentice* public house. There is a colony of grey heron nesting in the trees on Twickenham Ait, and this stretch of the river is well used by scullers.

After another half a mile, you arrive at Richmond Lock and Weir. Richmond Lock is half tidal; craft only need to use it when the weir is in position. At high tide, the weir is raised and craft can sail directly up the river; between half ebb and full tides the craft need to pass via the lock. Pass Richmond Lock, and then under Twickenham road and rail bridges. Follow the towpath into Richmond, under Richmond Bridge and past the jetties from which pleasure craft depart.

The path soon leaves the river and veers left into the River-side Gardens with the Terraced Gardens above to the left, under the road. A short detour into the Terraced Gardens is worthwhile. They were originally part of Buccleuch House on this site, and in the summer they are often used for theatrical performances. From the upper promenade one gets fine views over the Thames and six counties from Windsor to the North Downs. Returning to the original path, veer left to the far left-hand corner of the park where it meets the road near public conveniences. Join the road, passing forward for about 100 yards to cross it just past the Tudor Close Restaurant.

Traverse upwards, to the far right-hand corner of Peter-sham Common, emerging after 125 yards behind the Star and Garter Disabled Servicemen's Home. On the other side of the road, up the hill a little way, is the entrance to Richmond Park. Richmond Park was originally simply open ground with bushes, grassland and trees; it was enclosed by Charles I, who stocked it with red and fallow deer and engaged rangers to oversee it. After Charles's execution, it was given by Act of Parliament to 'the Mayor and Commonalty and Citizens of London and their Successors for ever'. Although the park has been used by successive members of royalty for shooting, public rights of way through it have never been challenged.

Motor traffic is banned at night and although pedestrians have right of access, the path is closed once or twice a year, merely to demonstrate that it is a concession rather than a right.

Enter the park through the imposing gates attributed to Lancelot (Capability) Brown, and when the road forks take the left fork, pass uphill and then down towards Bog Lodge where the Department of the Environment has administrative buildings. Cross the metalled road which leads up to the lodge and then climb to the left to a copse of young oaks and stumps of felled elms. Keeping parallel to the road on your right, continue forward for half a mile, crossing the metalled road which leads left to the Sheen Gate. Cross through a small wood and then around football pitches towards the high-rise flats which won a design award when they were constructed. Cross the Beverley Brook by either the road or footbridge and follow the road left to emerge at the Roehampton Gate.

Outside the gate, turn immediately left and follow a narrow alley between the brick wall of the park on your left and the fences of houses on your right. After 150 yards, after crossing the footbridge, turn immediately to your right and, continuing with the stream on your right and open ground on your left, you will soon see the Bank of England's Sports Ground on high ground to your right. Do not cross the footbridge towards this, but continue on this side of the stream through putting-greens and allotments, to emerge on Sunbury Avenue.

Bear right down Gilpin Avenue and cross Upper Richmond Road West to take Queen's Road which is slightly to the right. Follow Queen's Road to the end and then cross the railway using the footbridge. Take Avondale Road straight ahead, with the main entrance to the bus garage on your left. Crossing Mortlake High Street, a small grassed park gives access to the Thames and towpath.

Turn left, and walk upstream along the side of the brewery, past *The Ship* public house and under Chiswick Bridge, close to the finishing post for the University Boat Race. Continue past the drainage works and the new National Records Centre, under the railway bridge and back into Kew. Just before the bridge on the opposite bank is Strand on the Green, a delightful stretch of 18th- and 19th-century cottages.

SYON PARK — ISLEWORTH — RIVER THAMES TO ST. MARGARET'S AND MARBLE HILL — FERRY TO HAM HOUSE — PETERSHAM — RICHMOND — KEW — BRENTFORD — SYON PARK

8 miles or 5 miles

This is a civilised walk along both banks of the Thames between Syon Park and Marble Hill just above Richmond. The path is well made-up along the route. At the farthest upstream point a ferry operates during summer weekends. For the rest of the year it is necessary to cross at Richmond Bridge.

The walk passes open land for the greater part but the last mile back from Kew Bridge involves road walking, which can be rather tedious, and you may prefer to take a bus.

How to get there: By car — Parking available in Syon Park. By train — British Rail from Waterloo to Syon Lane and walk short distance to Syon Park. By bus — No. 117 from Shepherd's Bush or Hammersmith to Syon Park; No. 267 from Hammersmith or Hampton Court to Syon Park; E1 or E2 (Sundays) from Greenford to Syon Park. By underground — Piccadilly Line to Hounslow East, then bus No. 117 from the bus garage to Syon Park.

Syon Park is now in the care of the Department of the Environment, and stands on the site of an old Bridgettine nunnery founded by Henry V in 1415. During the dissolution of the monasteries in 1534 it passed to the Duke of Somerset, who was executed for treason in 1552. It was his house physician, Turner, who planted the original mulberry trees in the gardens, the descendants of which still bear fruit. Later, James I gave Syon to the Duke of Northumberland, with whose family it is mainly associated. After repairs in the 17th century, Robert Adam supervised minor renovations, and Capability Brown replanned the gardens. The house resembles Osterley House, in that it is planned as a square surrounding an open courtyard with a rotunda. It is worth visiting for its furniture, pictures and statues. The Long Gallery is especially notable. Also in Syon Park is the London Transport Collection of public transport vehicles, the National Gardening Centre (a display of British horticulture), a doll collection, restaurant and snack bar. The 'Great Conservatory', designed by Fowler in iron and glass, is reminiscent of those at Kew just across the river, although somewhat smaller.

Take the metalled road, leaving Syon Park at the main entrance and turn left outside the gates. Follow the road round to the right with the river on your left and the parish church of All Saints on your right. It is worth looking inside this church. Only the tower remains of the original 15th-century building. The rest is a tasteful 20th-century creation of dark Middlesex bricks and wood. The central altar stands directly below the inverted roof.

Continue along the road passing the *London Apprentice,* a famous 18th-century inn, on the left. This stands above Isleworth draw-dock, where boats and barges are hauled ashore for renovations. Follow Church Road, through bollards in the road and over a culvert at Mill Plait. The mill here has long since vanished.

Turn left after 150 yards at the junction with North Street and then left again at South Street along Richmond Road, passing Nazareth House on your left. Cross an outfall of the Crane River after 200 yards and then turn left down Railshead Road, past Maria Gray/Borough Road College to emerge at the river where houseboats are moored. Bear right along Isleworth Promenade towards Richmond Weir and Lock.

For the shorter walk, cross the footbridge at Richmond Weir and follow the main walk from Richmond Lock(*).

To continue on the main walk, follow this bank of the river, past Richmond Weir with the lock on the far side. The well-made pavement passes under Twickenham road and rail bridges before diverging from the river behind riverside dwellings along a path known as Duck's Walk. Carry straight ahead via Willoughby Road to Richmond Bridge after 300 yards. Staying on this side of the river, cross the road and take the slipway path down to the left back to the water's edge. Turn right and continue upstream past the recreation ground and the skating rink and follow the riverside path, to reach Marble Hill Park after a quarter of a mile. Marble Hill House was built around 1730 for Henrietta Howard, mistress of George II; the gardens were laid out by Bridgeman to a design suggested by a neighbour, Alexander Pope. Later, the house was occupied by another royal mistress, Mrs. Fitzherbert. From Marble Hill one can see over eight miles to Ham, Richmond Park and Wimbledon Common. The house is open to the public, every day except Friday.

Continue around the bend in the river, through a tunnel of trees, past allotments on the right, and emerge into a small park. Leave this via the gate in the far right-hand corner and bear left along the road to pass under an iron girder bridge at Riverside. Walk on past the back entrance to the Orleans Gallery. Just before the *White Swan* public house on the left, there is a ferry which operates at summer weekends only. Take this to Ham House on the opposite bank. The ferry is remarkable in that it is the only one on the river which still uses a wherry, the traditional rowing boat of the Thames watermen. If the ferry is not operating, then the best plan is to retrace your steps either back to the ferry plying from Marble Hill or further downstream to Richmond Bridge; cross at either of these points and rejoin the main walk.

On leaving the ferry, take the riverside path downstream in front of Ham House with the river on your left. Pass the point at which another ferry crosses the river from Marble Hill. Continue downstream with the river on your left for 200 yards past the track which joins from the right. Continue as Petersham Meadows open out to your right and then veer away from the river to the edge of a small park. Turn left into the park at the public conveniences and follow in front of a public house, boat sheds and snack bar to Richmond Bridge after a third of a mile.

Continue downstream with the river on your left towards Twickenham. Pass under Twickenham rail and road bridges and pass Richmond Lock as the Old Deer Park opens out to your right(*). Follow the towpath downstream with the river on your left for about two miles, passing first the golf course and then the Royal Botanical gardens, into Kew. Follow the river beside the car park and along the new flood wall for a further 250 yards to Kew Bridge.

Cross the river at Kew Bridge and turn left along the London Road in front of a large public house. From this point it is possible to take bus No. 117 or 267 back through Brentford to Syon Park. For those wishing to continue, there are several more points of interest. A short distance up the London Road on the opposite side is Kew Bridge Steam Engine Museum. The building was the first pumping station built to supply water from the Thames for use in London. It is now a museum housing the pumping equipment of that bygone Victorian era. It is also the home of several old steam traction engines. The whole thing can be seen 'in steam' at weekends from 11 a.m. to 5 p.m. Two hundred yards further up the London Road, just in front of Brentford Gas Works (again one of the first), is London's Piano Museum, housed in an old church. This comprises a unique collection of mechanical musical instruments including pianolas, polyphons, mechanical violins, and the only mechanical Wurlitzer in Europe. It is open on weekend afternoons.

It is another three-quarters of a mile back along the London Road, through Brentford High Street and so to Syon Park. If you have decided to walk this rather tedious stretch of road, pass through two sets of traffic lights, through the High Street and over the Grand Junction/Union Canal where it meets the Thames. You will pass Ferry Lane on the left. Where this lane meets the Thames there was originally a fortified ford, and there is a monument commemorating 54 BC when British tribesmen under Casivellanus bravely opposed the soldiers of Julius Caesar. Stakes thought to be the remains of underwater defences have been found in the river here. The monument also mentions that Offa held a council of the Church in Brentford in AD 780.

Continue along the London Road until just past the *George and Dragon* public house. Here, take the signposted alley back into Syon Park where we started.

CHISWICK (DUKE'S MEADOWS) — HAMMERSMITH BRIDGE — BARN ELMS PARK — BARNES COMMON — CHISWICK BRIDGE — DUKE'S MEADOWS

5½ miles or 4½ miles

This walk covers the section of river between Chiswick and Putney, the lowest stretch over which the towpath is now conveniently passable. Below Putney Bridge the river-side is built up and spoilt by major roads. Starting in the playing fields at Duke's Meadows, the walk follows the river past 18th-century houses and through small parks to Hammersmith Bridge. After crossing the river, it passes Barn Elms Reservoir and Barn Elms Park and then cuts back across Barnes Common to Chiswick Bridge. The Chiswick to Putney section of the river is where the Oxford *v* Cambridge Boat Race is run.

How to get there: By car — parking available in Duke's Meadows, just north of the railway line. By train — British Rail from Waterloo to Barnes Bridge and join the walk from there. By bus — any of the many frequent services to Hammersmith; start the walk at Hammersmith Bridge, following the instructions from there. By underground — Piccadilly, District or Metropolitan Lines to Hammersmith; start the walk from Hammersmith Bridge.

Leaving the car parked along one of the roads in Duke's Meadows, follow the river-bank downstream with the river on your right, along a path lined with weeping willows. Pass the bandstand and shelters on your left. At the end of Duke's Meadows, where rough ground starts, bear left away from the river by a small brick building. Follow a broad but disused metalled road for 200 yards, past a children's playing ground with railings on your right. When you reach the bowling green, turn right through a gap in the fence into the housing estate, making directly ahead for a telephone box. Here turn left to reach the main road after 75 yards. Bear across to the right to enter Corney Road, passing the end of Pumping House Lane.

Keep the cemetery on your right-hand side and enter it at the metal gates. Cross, using the paths, to the far left-hand corner in the direction of the church, and at the gate turn right onto a path which will bring you to the church after 25 yards. This is St. Nicholas' Church, the parish church of Chiswick, where Hogarth, William Kent and the third Earl of Burlington are buried. If the gates of the churchyard are locked, then make your way down Pumping House Lane to the far end and leave it through the bollards.

If you have time at this point you may wish to make a short detour to Chiswick House. If so, then on leaving the church-yard turn left instead of right and follow the path and, later, road up to the main road. Cross this to enter the grounds of Chiswick House. The house was originally built as a meeting place for Lord Burlington and his friends; it fell into disrepair and is now slowly being restored. Like many other houses in the west of London, it is built as a rotunda with an exterior stairway.

Hogarth's House, on the Hogarth Roundabout, Great West Road, is about 150 yards further up the Great Chertsey Road from the entrance to Chiswick House. It is open daily and contains many of Hogarth's famous prints: caricatures of 18th-century London life.

To continue the walk from the church, keep to the right-hand path on this side of the church, with the railings of the cemetery on your right. After 50 yards come to Pumping House Lane and turn left. Carry on past the bollards in the road with the church on your left to enter Chiswick Mall. Pass an island on your right and walk for 400 yards to where the Mall becomes Hammersmith Terrace — a row of sixteen identical houses built in 1750. Sir Alan Herbert used to live here. At the end of Hammersmith Terrace, follow the river through a small grassy plot with Chiswick Pumping Station, built in 1812, on the far side. Pass in front of the 17th-century *Ship* public house to enter the Upper Mall.

Pass the sailing club with boat-houses on the opposite bank of the river. At the far end of the Upper Mall is the house from which Sir Francis Ronalds constructed the first telegraph, eight miles long. Following the river, enter a small alleyway and pass the *Dove* public house on your right and the house where Thomas J. Coben Sanderson, a famous bookbinder, lived in the early 19th century. At the end of the alley, enter Furnivall Gardens, named after Doctor Furnivall, a noted man of letters. Bear slightly right, following the river past Hammersmith Pier.

In the 19th century, this area used to be known as The Creek and was a wharf for Thames barges bringing wares to and from Hammersmith. Just above this point used to stand a bridge known as the High Bridge. Follow the river towards Hammersmith Bridge, past rowing clubs and public houses. At the end of the terrace on the left is the headquarters of the amateur rowing association.

Climb the steps and cross Hammersmith Bridge to the far side. Descend to the towpath and pass under the bridge, walking downstream past Harrod's depository after 300 yards. Barn Elms waterworks is soon followed by the grass banks of the reservoir itself. On the opposite bank of the river is a new housing development in Fulham. Pass the monument to S. Fairbairne (founder of the Head of the River Race) at a point approximately one mile from the start of the boat race at Putney. Continue along the river path, past the entry gate to Barn Elms Park on the right. Pass Barn Elms boat-house on this bank and Fulham football ground opposite. Barn Elms Park was once the residence of Sir Francis Walsingham, Secretary of State to Elizabeth I.

At the far end of the park, cross the Beverley Brook by the footbridge and after 50 yards turn right into Ashlone Road, with a children's recreation ground on your left. Turn right again after 100 yards into Danemere Street and follow this street to the left to meet the main road. Here, turn right and then right again after 25 yards into a wide alleyway. At the end of this, turn left opposite Horne House and pass in front of Knox House towards a telephone box. Go straight past the telephone box, with the block of flats on your right, to come out on Barnes Common.

Follow the line of oak trees straight ahead, with a chapel across the common to your left. After 350 yards, pass tennis courts on your right and a second chapel and cemetery on your left. Cross the main road with public conveniences on your right, to the small metalled path directly opposite. Follow this for 300 yards, veering right as the common narrows, and the path crosses the Beverley Brook again at the white footbridge. Head for the pond directly ahead, with the church on your left.

Passing to the left of the pond, cross the road in front of the health centre and Essex Lodge, taking the left-hand fork in the road. Follow this road, with shops on either side, for 75 yards to meet the Thames floodwall again. Follow this upstream to your left.

Optional short cut: Cross the railway bridge 100 yards ahead, back to Duke's Meadows on the opposite bank, where we left the car.

To continue with the main walk, carry on along this bank of the river, under Barnes railway bridge, keeping to the water's edge. Pass behind *Ye White Hart* public house and soon, after a small park, head towards Chiswick Bridge in the distance. Pass under the shadow of the brewery, in front of *The Ship* public house, and then climb the stone steps to cross Chiswick Bridge. Descend the steps on the far Middlesex bank. On your left is the Promenade Allotment Estate; on your right is the river.

Continue along this bank towards the railway bridge. Pass a small car park and at the boat-houses, after a third of a mile of walking, follow the road as it bears left under the railway line. Follow it back into the northern part of Duke's Meadows where we parked the car.

WINDSOR GREAT PARK, BISHOP'S GATE — SNOW HILL — QUEEN ANNE'S RIDE — DUKE'S LANE — PRINCE CONSORT'S GATE — VIRGINIA WATER — SMITH'S LAWN — SAVILLE GARDENS — BISHOP'S GATE

7 miles

This is a walk around the perimeter of Windsor Great Park with wide views to the north over Windsor Castle. Most of it is along metalled paths which criss-cross the park and is therefore perfectly passable in wet weather. It passes through The Village, a small group of houses, before descending to Virginia Water. The route then passes the large polo field at Smith's Lawn and the obelisk pond, before returning to Bishop's Gate.

How to get there: By car — parking is available outside Bishop's Gate. Leave the A30 two miles south-west of Runnymede, just outside Egham. Turn right along Wick Lane and drive for approximately two miles. Turn left at Bishop's Gate and park anywhere near the *Fox and Hounds* public house. By train — British Rail from Waterloo to Egham. Then Green Line Bus No. 441 to Englefield Green. By bus — No. 441 Green Line from Staines to Englefield Green, or coach service No. 718 hourly from Victoria Coach Station, London, to Englefield Green.

Leaving the car near the *Fox and Hounds* public house, walk forward through Bishop's Gate towards the imposing white, double gate-houses of the Royal Lodge directly ahead. Just before reaching them, bear right and follow this metalled path round to the left along the hillside. As you bear further round you get magnificent views over Windsor and the castle. Descend over a walled section of road, ignoring the track from the left, and walk forward to where the broad and imposing Long Walk meets our track from the right. At this point it is probably worth climbing the hillside above and to your left, to the top of Snow Hill, where the Jubilee Firework Celebrations were held in 1977. On the summit is a statue of George III on horseback, and from here a tremendous panorama is visible. It is possible to see across Eton, Windsor Castle, the reservoirs of Datchet and Wraysbury, Runnymede, and Heathrow Airport to the Chilterns in the west and to trace the course of the Thames into the heart of London towards Battersea Power Station.

Return to the original track, past a copse originally planted in 1682, and continue winding round the hillside to the left. On the right, the ground slopes away into fields, and on the left are enclosed paddocks. At the fork in the road, bear right for 400 yards towards The Village. Where the track is joined by the broad Queen Anne's Ride coming in from the castle to your right, turn left, between houses.

Continue up this broad grassy ride with Windsor Castle behind you. The oak trees on either side are frequently heavy with mistletoe. After 100 yards cross the first road and rise to a second, meeting this after another 250 yards. Continue straight ahead along the ride, with a sports ground on your right, and rise to a road and fence marked 'Private Area' after one third of a mile. Turn left along the road and, keeping to the right-hand fence, veer right on to Duke's Lane with a house on your left-hand side. Follow Duke's Lane downhill, then rise past conifers on your left. Ignore the path into the private area on the left and continue along the main track. After three quarters of a mile in Duke's Lane, cross a small stream from a pond on the right, and start to climb uphill towards the Prince Consort's Gate. Keep to the left-hand fence and, one third of the way up the hill, turn left along the fence down a horse ride.

Pass through the iron gate after 150 yards and climb the stile at the next gate. Continue straight ahead for 400 yards to cross the next stile. Here, keep to the left bank of the stream, which is in fact the head stream of Virginia Water. Cross a small bridge and rise to the right with the ever widening expanse of water to your right. Follow this grassy track beside Virginia Water for one third of a mile to where the elaborate stone bridge carries the road from Blacknest Gate. Turn left here along the road and follow this for one third of a mile past Temple Cottage on the right, ignoring the junction from the left. Descend past the white fence which marks the road as it passes the water, where the upper lake descends to the lower one.

On the far side of the water, take the metalled path uphill to the left, signposted to the Cumberland Gate and Smith's Lawn. Half-way up this hill, where the main road bends to the left, carry straight on past a wooden barrier and through the rhododendrons. Take this track straight over the top of the hill to meet the edge of Smith's Lawn Polo Field. Here, bear right behind the club-house and spectators' stands, and follow this road as it bends left towards the cottage at the end of the field. Pass around the back of the cottage and follow the road downhill for 100 yards, through a copse of silver birches, to the bottom of the hill. Here veer left, along the path signposted to the Saville Gardens and Car Park. After 150 yards turn left along the near shore of the lake so that the water is on your right-hand side. Follow the dirt track between rhododendrons and past horse-jumps to the end of the lake.

Here, turn sharp right towards an obelisk and then sharp left with the perimeter fence of the Saville Gardens on your immediate left. Pass the entrance to the Saville Gardens restaurant and shops after 200 yards. At the end of the gardens, where the road rises to the left, carry straight on along a dirt track between tall rhododendrons. Cross the first crossroads and after 300 yards note the small lake to the left before the rhododendrons close in once more.

Ignore the track from the right after another 300 yards, but pass straight ahead, meeting a fence on the left and heading for the green gates ahead. Pass through the kissing-gate back into Windsor Great Park again, and bear right for 50 yards back to Bishop's Gate, outside which we left the car.

BLACK PARK — LANGLEY PARK — GRAND JUNCTION/UNION CANAL TO IVER — DELAFORD PARK — IVER HEATH — BLACK PARK

11½ miles

Both Black Park and Langley Park are well worth visiting. Black Park's natural lake, fringed with tall pine trees, is used at weekends by owners of model boats, and there is also a section reserved for swimming. Both parks are ideal for a Sunday afternoon stroll. This route starts in Black Park and passes through Langley Park, down to the Grand Union Canal. The two and a half mile walk along the canal is interesting and varied, especially the last half mile, where it crosses the Colne Brook and flooded gravel pits. From here we cross the Colne Brook through Iver Village to Delaford Park and thence to the high ground of Iver Heath with good views over Uxbridge. Passing close to Pinewood Film Studios, the route then re-enters the back of Black Park at Langley Corner.

How to get there: By car — parking is available in Black Park. Leave the A412 3 miles west of Uxbridge along Black Park Road, signposted to Wexham and Fulmer. By train — British Rail, Paddington to Langley and join the walk at Langley Station.

Leaving the car park in Black Park, head for the lake, crossing a wooden footbridge and then walking round the right-hand end of the lake towards the refreshment hut. Bear round the left-hand edge of the lake until you reach the lifebuoy, about 50 yards past the refreshment hut. Here, turn right away from the water up into the woods. Follow the track, joining a path from the right, which leads to the back of the warden's cottage. This path soon becomes a worn metalled road. Follow it for 150 yards and then bear right at a fork before leaving Black Park through the gates just before the warden's cottage.

At the end of the entrance drive, cross the main dual carriageway to the right to enter the main gates of Langley Park, almost directly opposite. There is a useful map just inside the gate.

Veer away from the main drive down a path half left. Descend into a copse of silver birches, cross a stream and then rise again, crossing a path onto an open field about 300 yards from the main gates. Ahead are public conveniences. Bear right, downhill, towards the house at the bottom of the field. At the bottom, after about 350 yards, pass an old barn on your left, now used as a Field Study Centre. In front of the barn, turn right, passing the gates into Langley House on your left. This is now a Conference Centre. Cross the main entrance road, heading downhill with pasture on your right and the house on your left.

After 250 yards, bear left round the head of the lake and pass through a double kissing-gate. Follow the lake to the far end (about 350 yards) and then going straight ahead, cross the stile by the map on a post. Turn left along a raised path between brambles and small trees. After 100 yards cross a small outflow from the lake by a wooden footbridge, and 75 yards further on, turn right, following the public footpath across fields in the direction indicated on the signpost. Head towards a line of trees and a caravan site. Pass the line of trees at a stile after 250 yards, and walking straight ahead enter an orchard. Keep to the path to meet a metalled track at a gate 250 yards further on.

Walk straight ahead towards pylons, through the caravan site. Ignore a road to the left. At the end of this track, follow a path slightly uphill through rough land. Pass under the power lines and between gravel pits to cross the bridge over the Grand Union Canal after 100 yards. Turn down left along the towpath on the far side of the canal. On your right across fields is the high-speed railway line to London from the West Country. On the opposite side of the canal are gravel workings. The route now follows the canal for 2½ miles.

After one third of a mile, pass under the first road bridge, close to Langley Station. Follow the canal past an oil terminal and factories on the right. On the far bank are moorings supervised by the Chandlery situated just before the next road bridge. Pass under this and then walk past the caravan site.

Then pass the vast storage yard of contractors' equipment on the right, just before passing another disused bridge. Keep to this bank, walking above the canal with rough ground opening out to the right.

Cross the next road directly into Court Lane beside the electricity sub-station. After 150 yards pass a farm and caravan park, continuing along the lane to its end, close to the point where a pipe and bridge cross the canal. Descend to the side of the canal again and walking forward all the time, follow the canal across a viaduct just before power lines. After 200 yards, cross another viaduct, then after 50 yards cross the canal to the opposite bank by the iron bridge carrying the bridleway. Follow this bridleway downhill through the copse for 150 yards to meet a lake. At the lake, bear left across the footbridge and keep right around the house into Ford Lane with the site of the old ford now behind you.

Follow Ford Lane for 300 yards to the main road with the flooded gravel pit on your left and glimpses of Iver Church on high ground also to the left. Pass under power lines and past a farm on the right. At the end of Ford Lane, cross the main road and follow the public footpath through the gate, over the river and round to the left in front of an old house. After 75 yards, turn right, and uphill again at the main road. Pass the church on the opposite side of the road and then *The Swan* and *The Bull* public houses in Iver Village. After 150 yards, pass a Methodist chapel on the right, and 75 yards further on, turn right into Bangors Road South, signposted to Iver Heath. Walk along this winding road for 400 yards, before turning right into The Coppins (a cul-de-sac), at a left-hand bend in the road. Follow the metalled road and the brick wall of the house on your left; note the folly. Two hundred yards further on, pass cottages on the right with views of Uxbridge ahead through the trees. The metalled track bears right into a farm, but continue straight ahead, downhill along the dirt path.

Pass through an iron gate to the house at the bottom of the hill. Cross the bridge to the left, following the road for 25 yards. Cross the stile in the left-hand fence and walk with the lake on your right-hand side and the river on your left, around the headland and to the left of the sailing club compound. Cross the stile, keeping to the river, and take the track on the far side of the compound. After 100 yards cross the river to the left, and follow the road, turning sharp right; 150 yards after crossing the river, traverse rough ground to the right towards two pylons. Follow the river to the left for 150 yards, upstream to the bridge. Here, turn left, uphill along the road for one third of a mile.

At the top of the hill, the road veers to the left. Take the public footpath on the right-hand side of the road, opposite a post box; cross the stile and follow the path across fields. Descend to a second stile after 200 yards. Cross this and continue between fences, along the rear of houses to emerge on Bangors Road North, opposite a cul-de-sac. Turn right for 200 yards to the main road (A412). Cross the main road (Denham Road) to the footpath directly opposite. Follow this along the rear of houses, descending to a stream and then climbing uphill with a field to the right. Where the houses end, continue forward and slightly to the right, through the remains of old gate-posts. Follow the path straight along the hedge, crossing three small fields. Rise to the brow of the hill, and with a small circular copse to your left, descend to the road.

At the road, turn left and follow it for half a mile, past the caravan site and Cherry Orchard Farm, noting the Pinewood Film Studios across fields to the left. Ignore the public foot-path to the right and follow the road, walking along the verges. At Langley Corner, cross over, slightly towards the right. Here you will find a useful map and direction indicator. Take the path just inside the woods which follows the road to Fulmer and Gerrards Cross on the right.

After 200 yards, directly opposite the Bridgettine Guest House, where the road veers to the right, take the main track to the left into Black Park. Pass through young plantations for 250 yards to a place where seven paths meet. Take the second path on the right and continue on this, crossing two paths at right angles to emerge at Black Park Lake after about half a mile. Bear right along the lake back to the car park.

UXBRIDGE — GRAND JUNCTION/UNION CANAL TO HAREFIELD — BAYHURST COUNTRY PARK — GRAND UNION CANAL — UXBRIDGE

9 miles

This walk follows the valley of the river Colne, along the river and the Grand Union Canal. After passing through flooded gravel pits, used by anglers and yachters and abounding with waterfowl, the walk leaves the river at Mount Pleasant. It then rises to the top of the valley side, through pasture and arable land to Bayhurst Wood Country Park. From here, it gradually descends back to the canal and thence to Uxbridge once more. Boots or strong shoes are recommended.

How to get there: By car — Turn off the A40 on to the B467 to Uxbridge. Turn right with the B467 and follow it (now Harefield Road) for 300 yards to the *Arbrook Arms* public house. Cars may be parked here (with landlord's permission) or on the land to the right of the pub, marked to the Alderglade–Uxbridge Nature Reserve. By underground: Piccadilly or Metropolitan Line to Uxbridge. Leave the centre of the town along Harefield Road and walk for just over half a mile to the *Arbrook Arms* on the left. By bus — No. 207 Shepherd's Bush to Uxbridge; No. 222 Hounslow to Uxbridge. Alight at Underground Station and follow directions from there.

Leave the *Arbrook Arms* and follow the dirt track down to the right of the public house along the side of the river (marked to the Alderglade–Uxbridge Nature Reserve). After 200 yards, cross the river by the footbridge to the far bank and turn right along the waterside. Bear to the left of the house 200 yards further on and pass under the disused railway line. Turn right and follow the fenced path under the elevated part of the A40. **Do not** cross the stile directly ahead, but keep along the fence to the left towards the white bridge visible across the field.

Cross the bridge and turn right so that the canal is now on your right. After about a quarter of a mile rise to Denham Lock No. 87; just after the lock, the bed of the canal is built up to allow the river Colne to flow under it, which is an interesting feat of engineering. Continue walking alongside the canal, under the electricity pylons, to bridge No. 182. As you pass under this, you will be aware of flooded gravel pits on either side, some used as yachting basins. Others are frequented by anglers and the whole area is noted for its waterfowl.

Pass under the railway viaduct and walk for a further half mile to bridge No. 180, just before which a break in the opposite bank allows river craft to moor in one of the flooded pits. At bridge No. 180 there is a public house for the thirsty. Suitably refreshed, pass under the road to Widewater Lock, No. 86. Walk for a further half mile with gravel pits on your left, noting a small island of reeds on the right-hand side of the canal. Pass under bridge No. 179, as the land widens out into fields with a hill to the right. Over the hill to the left is Denham Aerodrome, so do not be surprised by the swarms of private light aircraft. Follow the curve of the canal as it sweeps first left and then right to bridge No. 178. Here, at the Mill Restaurant, we leave the canal, and crossing the bridge, start to rise uphill. After 25 yards, turn to the right at the T-junction, 50 yards further on the road turns sharply left and continues uphill. (It is easier to follow the road, rather than the public footpath which is marked over the stile and then uphill to the left. A little further on this path is easily lost on the edge of some recent buildings. However, for those who are determined, it is possible to find the way through to the main road and then to turn right.) For those choosing to keep to the road, turn left and uphill. At the more major road, turn right for 300 yards to cross-roads. Here turn right to South Harefield. Keep along the road for half a mile and then bear left along the metalled track to Harefield parish church, slightly downhill. Ignore the public footpath signposted to the left, and pass straight forward in front of the church and the Australian Military Cemetery.

Fifty yards further on, at the meeting of three paths, turn right for 25 yards to a gap in the hedge on the left and cross the stile. Bear diagonally to the left to meet a second stile after 150 yards. Cross this and, keeping the hedge on your left, come to the first gate. Here, turn right and start to walk uphill, to the next public footpath sign at the left of a large farm. Keeping to the left of the hedge, walk uphill to the next stile and signpost.

Cross this stile, and then walk across the large field to the far left-hand corner, keeping either to its edges or to the path which crosses directly. In the far corner, cross the stile and then walk through the small, narrow thicket or along the edge of the next field for 100 yards. Pass a house on the left and cross an open wide path to yet another stile. Cross this and, keeping the hedge on your left, pass under the electricity cables, walking uphill to the tall trees 200 yards directly ahead. On your left, is a Nature Reserve belonging to the Hertford-shire and Middlesex Naturalists' Trust. In front, the tall trees mark the beginning of Bayhurst Wood Country Park.

Cross the stile and turn immediately to the right. With the barbed-wire fence on your right, continue along the edge of the wood for about a third of a mile, past the first stile on the right. In wet weather there may be a small area of flooded meadow to the right, close to a temporary footpath sign. At this point cross the stile on the right and keep alongside the hedge to the left. (If you reach the public picnic place and you are still inside the perimeter fence you have gone too far.) After 300 yards you will come to a double stile on the left. **Do not cross this**, but continue in the same direction as before with the hedge on your left. Continue uphill, crossing several tree trunks set into the ground as stepping stones, and emerge after 100 yards on to the road.

Turn right along the road, ignoring the public footpath signs. Pass under the electricity cables and after 75 yards turn left, uphill by the side of the caravan site along the bridleway. Climb to the top of the hill, past a bungalow on the left, and then start to descend again, following the muddy path used by many horses. After a quarter of a mile pass the Glaxo Farm on your right and emerge at the main road.

Here, turn right under the railway bridge for 100 yards, to take the public footpath marked on the right. Turn along this, past Brackenbury Farm. Where caravans and trailers are parked, bear to the left through a rustic fence towards an iron gate. Here keep left along the side of the hedge to an open field. Cross the broken wooden fence and keep to the right-hand side of the field. Continue in this direction, crossing a further three stiles, and proceed across open fields for about a quarter of a mile, until you meet the metalled road. Cross this and climb over another stile. Bear to the left for 75 yards across open ground to arrive at the golf links. Looking down-hill and to the left it is possible to see the flooded gravel pits for which we are heading.

Take the main path through the golf links, downhill. Keep to the path, which is well marked. Follow this public footpath to the gravel pits, with water on both sides. Here there are many interesting waterfowl and the shores are lined with tall bullrushes. Continue past the second pair of lakes back to the canal at bridge No. 182. Turn left back along the canal, using either bank. Pass lock No. 87, where the river flows under the canal, and at bridge No. 183, where we initially joined the canal, turn left, back over the fields, under the A40 and the disused railway bridge and along the river, back to the car or into Uxbridge to the station.

SYON PARK — BRENTFORD DOCK — GRAND JUNCTION/UNION CANAL TO NORWOOD GREEN — OSTERLEY PARK — GRAND JUNCTION CANAL TO SYON PARK

8 miles

This walk follows the Grand Junction/Union Canal from Syon Park through Brentford Dock and up the steepest section of the canal where it climbs out of the Thames basin at Hanwell. From there it cuts across Osterley Park and back to the canal for the return journey.

How to get there: By car — parking is available at Syon Park. By train — British Rail from Waterloo to Syon Lane Station and walk to Syon Park. By bus — No. 117 from Shepherd's Bush or Hounslow East to Syon Park; No. 267 from Hammersmith or Hampton Court to Syon Park.

Leave Syon Park in the opposite direction from the main entrance, with the Gardening Centre and London Transport Collection on your right. Proceed along the pedestrian path with tall walls on either side for 100 yards, passing a small recreation ground on your left. After passing through a small housing development meet the London Road and turn right. At a bend, after about 100 yards, cross the London Road and enter Brentford Wharf where Commerce Way and the Grand Junction Canal meet the main road.

The Brentford to Uxbridge section of this tremendous engineering feat was opened in November 1794 and by 1800 the whole of its London to Midlands route had been completed at a total cost of one million pounds. The main line is ninety-three miles long, thus shortening the previously used route along the Oxford Canal and the Thames by sixty miles. The canal itself is forty-two feet wide, four and a half feet deep, and its one hundred and two locks were designed to take barges up to seventy-two feet in length. Until 1838, when Robert and George Stevenson's steam railway was opened, it was the main link carrying coke, coal, hay, pottery, bricks and limestone to London and taking away manure, ashes and finished products.

With the advent of the railway, the importance of the canal declined so that today it is used mainly for heavy timber and building materials. There is also a pleasure craft centre based at Brentford. In 1929 the Grand Junction Canal Company merged with the Grand Union Canal Company.

Follow the path on to Brentford Lock No. 100. Keep to the left of the water where lighters are moored and pass over a movable wooden walkway. The path leads under a covered wharf with sides of corrugated iron and at the far end goes out under a railway bridge. Follow the towpath as it curves under the Great West Road and into the industrial estate. Climb slightly to the next lock, No. 99 (Clitheroe's or New Brentford Lock) which has a fall of 7 feet 7 inches. On the right, through rushes, a small stream enters. Passing close to the elevated section of the M4 motorway, cross the canal by the iron bridge built by Horsley and Company in 1820. Pass under the underground railway bridge and the motorway, continuing along the towpath to where a stream enters around a wooded island.

Cross at Osterley Lock, No. 98, which has a 5 foot 6 inch fall, and soon pass over the weir by the wood and iron gantry. Pass the section of the canal which in 1959 won the Kerr Prize for pile-driving, and then the Sea Cadets' headquarters on the right. Note the road bridge here as this is the point where we rejoin the canal on the return journey. After continuing along the path for another third of a mile, cross a road by a small brick bridge. There is next a flight of locks, the Hanwell Flight, which together take the canal out of the steepest part of the Thames basin. Note the small reservoirs on the opposite bank, used for conserving water when the canal was in heavy use. At the first lock a small stream to the right leads away to join the river Brent and the Paddington branch. Pass behind the new King Edward Hospital and St. Bernard's Psychiatric Hospital.

The bridge just ahead marks Three Bridges, where the canal crosses the railway by a metal viaduct and the road crosses the canal. Follow the path under the bridge and pass the first lock after 150 yards. Another 150 yards will bring you under a white bridge to Norwood Top Lock, No. 90. Here cross the white bridge, and keeping straight ahead, come out on to Melbury Avenue and bear right after 50 yards. Follow this to its end and then turn left into Minterne Avenue. One hundred yards further on, turn right into Tentelow Lane with fields on your left. Follow Tentelow Lane for 250 yards, bearing to the right in the direction of *The Plough* public house. Just before *The Plough* there is a narrow track on the left, starting by the entrance to the saloon bar. Take this, with the garden of the pub on your right and a bowling green on your left. After about 50 yards cross over the cul-de-sac and take the path directly opposite between houses Nos. 32 and 34. After 50 yards emerge onto an open field. Cross this diagonally left, heading for the bridge visible in the distance. At the other side of the field climb a few stone steps and cross a stile before taking Osterley Lane to the left and crossing the road bridge over the M4 motorway. Follow this road for 100 yards before turning right past Devon Lodge to enter the back of Osterley Park. Continue down the path for a quarter of a mile until you emerge on the lawn in front of Osterley House.

Of the original house built in 1577 by Sir Thomas Gresham, founder of the London Stock Exchange and Gresham College, only the stable block (now tea rooms) and the walled kitchen garden remain. The rest is contained within Robert Adam's 18th-century conversion. The house was originally built with four towered sides around a central courtyard. Adam altered the house to transform the first floor into the main living accommodation according to the Italian *piano nobile* principle, and added an elaborate raised Ionic portico on the fourth side. The lakes and the Doric temple were present in the original grounds but Adam added the conservatory and remodelled the gardens. Many of his original plans are on show, together with furniture, tapestries and paintings, all in their original setting. The Etruscan Room, inspired by the art of Pompeii, is especially worth visiting.

After looking around or perhaps visiting the house, continue directly ahead, taking the main exit path. Pass between two ponds, the higher on your right. The metalled road from the car park has paths on both sides and tall trees form a protective canopy. Just past the cottages, half way out and on the far side of a wooden fence, there is an iron kissing-gate on the left. Take the path through this gate and, after walking about 200 yards with fields on both sides, turn sharp right through another gate. Walk for 100 yards to the backs of large houses and turn left with fields on your left and the houses on your right. After 300 yards you will come out on to a grassed area. Carry straight on with a wall on your left, past the double gate-house at the side of Osterley Park. Bear left to come out on to Windmill Lane.

Walk along the road and pass *The Hare and Hounds* public house. Go under the motorway and walk uphill for about 200 yards. Here, on the right-hand side of the road, a high wire fence encloses the playing fields of Warren Farm School. Immediately before this, by the side of a locked metal gate is a rusty iron kissing-gate which gives access to a narrow grassed track. Follow this downhill for 150 yards to the railway line and **cross carefully by the path**. This line is not electrified, and is used infrequently since it is simply a branch line to factories along the Grand Union Canal.

On the far side of the railway is part of a factory estate. Take the road going straight ahead, with a container depot on your left. Cross the canal by the road bridge and descend on the far side to rejoin the towpath. Retrace your steps down the canal to Brentford and Syon Park, first passing the Sea Cadets' headquarters and the pile-driving prize section of the canal.

SOUTHALL — GRAND JUNCTION/UNION CANAL TO BULL'S BRIDGE — PADDINGTON BRANCH TO HORSENDEN HILL — HANWELL — CANAL TO SOUTHALL

13 miles

This walk is mainly along the bank of the canal: part of the main line and a large section of the Paddington Branch. Although much of it passes through industrial areas and is therefore not so attractive, it is extremely interesting. Since the Paddington Branch follows the 100-foot contour around the edge of the Thames basin, there are many points along the walk where views over London are very impressive. The panorama from Horsenden Hill is probably the most effective in west London. From Horsenden Hill the walk returns to the canal at Hanwell through parks and minor roads.

How to get there: By car — limited parking is available on minor roads bordering the A3005 near Norwood Green, and along minor roads bordering the canal between Norwood Green and Southall. By train — British Rail from Paddington to Hanwell and join the walk at the railway viaduct, Hanwell. By bus — No. 207 from Shepherd's Bush to Southall Garage; No. 208 from Hayes to Southall Garage (Mondays to Fridays only); No. 83 from Golders Green and Wembley to Southall Garage. From Southall Bus Garage, cross the road to the right and take Windmill Lane to the right for 200 yards to Three Bridges. Pass under the road at Three Bridges. Continue along the towpath with the water on your left-hand side up to Norwood Green Lock. Pass under another road bridge, past Norwood Top Lock, to arrive at *The Lamb* public house.

Descend to the towpath at *The Lamb* public house, where the A3005 crosses the Grand Union Canal just north of Heston and Norwood Green. Walk under the canal bridge in a westerly direction. After 200 yards cross a footbridge under which a side branch passes into a private dock, just before a timber yard on the opposite bank. You will soon come upon houses on the far bank and then pass under bridge No. 202 just before the *Old Oak Tree* public house on the right.

Keep to the towpath beside the road with a recreation ground close by. After half a mile walk under another road bridge just before the *Grand Junction Arms* on the right. On the opposite side of the canal is North Hyde wharf, now another timber yard but once a busy munitions depot. Soon the towpath joins the road and a short distance brings you past moorings for houseboats and the British Waterways Board, to Bull's Bridge where the Paddington line starts. Directly ahead is the tall tower of the new electricity generating station. About 100 yards past Bull's Bridge the river Crane passes under the canal towards Cranford Park; the canal is supported by an aqueduct at this point. At Bull's Bridge, turn to the right to follow the Paddington line along its right-hand bank; you will soon pass the canal keeper's cottage.

Pass allotments on the left and after 400 yards walk under the railway bridge. Cross a bridge over a side inlet; pass the gas-works on your right, and an overflow into the Yeading Brook on the opposite bank, and then over another side inlet. Pass a pipeline; you will soon come to allotments on the right, and then follow the path along the rear of a row of houses. Keep to the towpath under the A4020 road bridge, passing the Territorial Army base and contractors' offices. A quarter of a mile further on, pass under a small metal bridge with a recreation ground on your right and fields on your left. Continue for one mile, and then pass under a gantry, and the B455, veering right under another road bridge 200 yards further on.

In a further 200 yards the canal curves left and then right. Harrow on the Hill is to the left about 3 miles away, and Horsenden Hill is 2 miles directly ahead. Pass under the A40 road bridge, with houseboats moored opposite, and then under the iron bridge of the tube-line. A further 100 yards brings you to an attractive factory estate. Cross the footbridge and then walk under another road bridge as the canal bends to the left. Soon the A4127 crosses the canal by a pub on the right-hand side.

Follow the canal as it curves right and then left with a golf course on the right-hand side and Horsenden Hill beyond pylons across sports fields to the left. Continue for 350 yards, where at the end of the golf course there is a concrete footbridge over the canal. A short detour from here to the top of Horsenden Hill is strongly recommended for the view. Cross the concrete footbridge, under the power lines and across the two playing fields and road and climb to the top of the hill.

Return to the concrete bridge. Maintaining your original direction, turn right down a small path between fences with the new IBM Computer Centre on your left and the golf course on your right. After 200 yards, at the club-house, turn right into Rockware Avenue and at the end turn left under the bridge. After 25 yards turn left into Bennett's Avenue and then take the first turning on the right — Middleton Gardens. Walk down this road for 300 yards through the one-way section and then turn left into Daynston Drive. At the end turn right onto Western Avenue, and cross this by the footbridge slightly to the left.

Descending from the footbridge in a westerly direction on the far side (i.e. away from the railway line), turn left almost immediately into Perivale Park, signposted *Hanwell 2 miles* by the Brent River Preservation Society. Seventy-five yards inside the park, turn right along the metalled path with the major part of the playing fields to your left and a tennis court on your right. Walk for 350 yards to a bowling green. Here, veer left across the grass, keeping to this side of the stream and ignoring the two footbridges. Keeping the stream on your right, meet a metalled track from the centre of the park and follow this to the right, over a footbridge to the gates of the park at Coston's Lane.

Turn left, following the Brent River across a small grass verge to the left and then walking onto the bridge carrying the Ruislip road, B455. Turn left along the main road for 150 yards, crossing it to take a footpath to the right, between fences, signposted *Hanwell 1 mile*. This path passes between playing fields for 150 yards before emerging onto Brookbank Avenue where you turn right. (There are plans for a right of way along the river; although an informal path exists, it is not yet listed as a public footpath.)

Continue down Brookbank Avenue as it becomes Bridge Avenue. At the end turn right for 20 yards and then turn left at the school into High Lane. After 100 yards, where the road bends to the left into Studland Road, carry straight ahead down the track prohibited to motor vehicles. With the Brent Valley Golf Course on either side, continue along this track and up the hill. At the top, turn right into Church Road, signposted *Hanwell Church ¼ mile*, and after 75 yards cross to the left at the corner of Churchfields Recreation Ground.

From here, cross diagonally left to the children's play area and the wooden shelter, and then veer left again to leave the park at Manor Court Road. After 50 yards turn right into Alwyne Road; bear to the right and head for the viaduct. Descend under the railway viaduct. Enter the sunken park on the right immediately after the viaduct and cross to the bottom left-hand corner. Leave the park and emerge onto Half Acre Road. At the end of Half Acre Road, with the pub on your right, cross the Broadway to the right into Lower Boston Road. After 150 yards turn right down Green Lane, passing the Victoria Hospital and *The Fox* public house on your right. At the end of Green Lane meet the Grand Union Canal again.

Turn right up the canal with the water on your left-hand side. Pass the Hanwell Flight (series of locks) with the new King Edward Hospital and St. Bernard's Hospital beyond the wall to your right. Pass under the road at Three Bridges where the road crosses the canal, which in turn crosses the railway. (If you started the walk from Southall Bus Garage you have now returned to your starting point.)

Continue along the towpath with the water on your left-hand side up to Norwood Green Lock. Pass under another road bridge, past Norwood Top Lock to return after a third of a mile to *The Lamb* public house where we started.

WIMBLEDON COMMON — BEVERLEY BROOK — RICHMOND PARK — ISABELLA PLANTATION — WIMBLEDON COMMON

6 miles

The Beverley Brook, which runs from Morden Park into the Thames just above Putney Bridge, flows down a river valley between Wimbledon Common in the east and Coombe Hill and Richmond Park in the west. This walk starts by Caesar's Camp on Wimbledon Common, a Roman settlement preserved as a site of historical importance, and from here descends to the Beverley Brook. This is followed to the Robin Hood Gate where the route enters Richmond Park. A circular route inside the park, through the Isabella Plantation and past the Pen Ponds and White Lodge, is followed by a return to Wimbledon Common.

How to get there: By car — Parking is available around Camp Road or Camp View off West Side Common on the south-east side of Wimbledon Common (off the B281). By train — From London, Victoria to Wimbledon Station and then bus No. 200 from the station to Wimbledon Common.

With Camp View directly behind you, take the lane past the club-house of Wimbledon Golf Club on your left. Keep to the lane for 300 yards to where it branches to the right and left. Walk straight ahead, taking a narrow path between wire fences down into the golf course and passing through the site of Caesar's Camp. Note the monument to the right of the path. Meander downhill between these fences with good views over Kingston, Coombe Hill and Richmond Park. Coombe Hill was the source of the spring tapped by Cardinal Wolsey when he piped water into Hampton Court.

After approximately 400 yards, cross the path from Warren Farm and pass through the gap in the fence immediately opposite. Walk downhill for approximately 75 yards past a stile and towards the bridge 50 yards further on. **Do not cross**

the bridge but turn right and, keeping the river on your left-hand side, follow it downstream with playing fields on the opposite bank. Follow this path on the right-hand bank for about a third of a mile and then cross the river just after a brick cottage on the opposite bank. After crossing the brick bridge, turn right and, with the river on your right-hand side, continue downstream, shortly passing a brick gauging station. After passing playing fields on the left, follow the path to the far end of the playing fields, veering left away from the river. Pass a metal barrier and a horse-riding circle and, keeping left, emerge on the A3 main road by white posts.

Cross the main road and enter Richmond Park through Robin Hood Gate directly opposite; 75 yards further on is a cross-roads. Follow the road directly ahead, marked *No Through Road – to Pen Ponds*, for 25 yards only and then bear left uphill, following the left-hand horse ride about 100 yards from the road. Pass Prince Charles's Spinney to the right and, on reaching the brow of the hill after a quarter of a mile, note Gibbet Wood on the right. To the left, at the top of the hill, is a car park and from this runs a path to the Isabella Plantation to your right. Continue straight ahead over the brow of the hill until you reach this path which is lined with park benches. On reaching it, follow it to the right and enter the Isabella Plantation at the perimeter gate. Our route follows the stream directly ahead, emerging at the far side of the plantation, but it is possible to take any of the paths, provided you return to the stream at the far end.

At the lower end of the plantation the small stream enters Peg's Pond. Leave the plantation, with this pond to your right, through the small gate and follow the road directly ahead for 75 yards to a T-junction. Here, turn right, immediately veering away from the road to the left, towards the left-hand end of the enclosed Pond Plantation, a quarter of a mile away. Follow one of the many deer-paths, picking up a small rivulet which is in fact the start of the second tributary of the Beverley Brook. On reaching Pond Plantation, keep the trees on your right-hand side and walk around the perimeter fence until the upper of the two Pen Ponds comes into view. In common with many other small ponds in the park, these are both disused gravel pits.

Walk directly ahead past both ponds. At the lower end of the second pond, turn right along its lower side, past the outflow, bearing uphill to the left along a wide ride towards White Lodge, with an open plantation on your left. Keeping the wooden fence of the lodge on your left, cross the metalled road and continue to the brow of the hill where fine views can be had over Roehampton and Putney. Continue straight ahead over the open space at the brow of the hill and then down into Spanker's Hill Wood. Pass a small pond in the lower part of the wood and veer half right. Coming out of the wood, pass a small enclosed area of young trees to your right and continue straight ahead towards the Robin Hood Gate between an ever-narrowing junction of roads. Pass a car park and leave Richmond Park by the Robin Hood Gate. Cross the road at the equestrian crossing point.

Follow the horse-ride directly down and cross the brick bridge over the river. Just before the sports ground, turn right along the river on your right-hand side, with playing fields on your left. Follow the track to where it leaves the playing fields and enters the woods. A footbridge crosses the river from the right at this point. Leave the track here and turn uphill to the left, crossing another track after 50 yards and then using a small wooden footbridge to cross a ditch. Keep uphill, aiming to stay on the main path without much deviation either to left or right. The dirt path soon becomes easier and after a quarter of a mile leaves the woods as the open ground of Wimbledon Common appears.

At the major path, turn right, through the golf course and, keeping straight ahead, after a quarter of a mile pass a monument to the King's Royal Rifle Corps who trained on the common during the First World War. Two hundred yards further on pass a white bungalow on your right-hand side, and veering slightly right, cross a dirt road towards the tall house on the corner of Camp View, near where we parked the car.

Also in this series:

Walks in the Surrey Hills
Walks in the Hills of Kent
Walks in Berkshire
Walks in the Cotswolds
Walks in Oxfordshire
Walks in Devon
Walks Along the Ridgeway
Walks Along Offa's Dyke
Walks in the Yorkshire Dales
Walks in Hampshire
Walks in Buckinghamshire
Walks in Sussex
Afoot in Hertfordshire
Walks in Avon
Afoot in Surrey
Walks in the Peak District
Walks in the Lake District
Walks in Exmoor

Every walker should read the following Venture Guides:

Map and Compass
Outdoor First Aid
Weather Lore
Hill Walking
Backpacking